Best Garden Plants *for* Washington *and* Oregon

Marianne Binetti • Don Williamson

LONE PINE INTERNATIONAL

LONE PINE PUBLISHING INTERNATIONAL

The Distributor: Lone Pine Publishing
1808 B Street NW, Suite 140
Auburn, WA, USA 98001

Website: www.lonepinepublishing.com

Library and Archives Canada Cataloguing in Publication

Williamson, Don, 1962-
    Best garden plants for Washington and Oregon / Don Williamson,
Marianne Binetti.

Includes index.
ISBN-13: 978-1-55105-506-0. ISBN-10: 1-55105-506-6

    1. Plants, Ornamental--Washington (State) 2. Plants, Ornamental--Oregon.
3. Gardening--Washington (State) 4. Gardening--Oregon. I. Binetti, Marianne,
1956- II. Title.

SB453.2.W3W54 2005   635.9'09797   C2004-905746-4

Photography: All photos by Tim Matheson and Tamara Eder except AA Selection 33a; Sandra Bit 143a; Karen Carriere 50a, 70a; Therese D'Monte 149b; Don Doucette 107b&c, 136b; Derek Fell 11a, 149a, 161a&b; Erika Flatt 9b, 145b, 167b, 171a&b; Chris Graham/Royal Botanical Gardens 131a; Anne Gordon 139b; Horticolor 135b; Duncan Kelbaugh 145a; Liz Klose 152a, 153a&b, 158a, 162a, 168a&b, 172a; Deborah Knapke 139a; Colin Laroque 78b; Dawn Loewen 83a; Heather Markham 78a; Marilynn McAra 148a; Kim O'Leary 74a, 97a, 147a, 155b; Allison Penko 10, 52a, 79b, 95b, 101b, 103a&b, 106b, 131b, 134b, 142b, 163a&b, 164a, 165b, 166a, 169a&b, 172b; Perennial Plant Association 62a; Laura Peters 9c, 143b, 151a&b, 152b, 155a, 156a&b, 157a&b, 158b, 160a, 162b, 164b, 165a, 167a, 170a&b; Robert Ritchie 46b, 123a; Saxon Holt 77a&b, 91, 117a; Leila Sidi 150b; Joy Spurr 132a, 135b; Peter Thompstone 22a, 25a, 30a, 53a, 54a, 58a, 65a, 69a, 70b; Don Williamson 146a&b.

Scanning & Electronic Film: Elite Lithographers Co.

Hardiness zones map: based on the USDA Plant Hardiness Zone Map

This book is not intended as a "how-to" guide for eating garden plants. No plant or plant extract should be consumed unless you are certain of its identity and toxicity and of your potential for allergic reactions.

PC: P1

Table of Contents

We would thank the following for their valuable time and beautiful images:
All-America Selections, Brad Jalbert, Colin Laroque, Dawn Loewen, Debra
Knapke, Don Doucette, Duncan Kelbaugh, Erika Flatt, Heather Markham,
Karen Carriere, Laura Peters, Liz Klose, Peter Thompstone, the Perennial
Plant Association, the Royal Botanic Gardens, Sandra Bit and all who
allowed us to photograph their gardens.

Introduction

Starting a garden can seem like a daunting task. Which plants should you choose? Where should you put them in the garden? This book is intended to give beginning gardeners the information they need to start planning and planting gardens of their own. It describes a wide variety of plants and provides basic planting information such as where and how to plant.

Washington and Oregon exhibit a diversity of ecological regions, each with its own unique challenges. Each region has a temperature range that indicates relative hardiness. Consider this: 5° F (−15° C) is very different with snow cover or without; in soggy soil or in dry; following a hot summer or a long, cold, wet one. These factors will have more influence on the survival of plants than will temperature. Recognizing the type of climate in which you garden will help you determine hardiness. Your local garden center should be able to provide you with local hardiness zones and frost date information.

Hardiness zones and frost dates are two terms often used when discussing climate. Hardiness zones consider the temperatures and conditions in winter. Plants are rated based on the zones in which they grow successfully. The last frost date in spring combined with the first frost date in fall helps us predict the length of the growing season.

Getting Started

When planning your garden, start with a quick analysis of the garden as it is now. Plants have different requirements and it is best to put the right plant in the right place rather than to change your garden to suit the plants you want.

Knowing which parts of your garden receive the most and least amounts of sunlight will help you choose the proper plants and decide where to plant them. Light is classified into four basic groups: full sun (direct, unobstructed light all or most of the day); partial shade (direct sun for about half the day and shade for the rest); light shade (shade all or most of the day with some sun filtering through to ground level); and full shade (no direct sunlight). Most plants prefer a certain amount of light, but many can adapt to a range of light levels.

Plants use the soil to hold themselves upright, but also rely on the many resources it holds: air, water, nutrients, organic matter and a host of microbes. The particle size of the soil influences the amount of air, water and nutrients it can hold. Sand, with the largest particles, has lots of air space and allows water and nutrients to drain quickly. Clay, with the smallest particles, is high in nutrients but has very little air space. Water is therefore slow to penetrate clay and slow to drain from it.

Soil acidity or alkalinity (measured on the pH scale) influences the nutrients available to plants. A pH of 7 is neutral; a lower pH is more acidic. Most plants prefer a soil with a pH of 5.5–7.5. Soil testing kits are available at most garden centers, and soil samples can be sent to testing facilities for a more thorough analysis.

Compost is one of the best and most important amendments you can add to any type of soil. Compost improves soil by adding organic matter and nutrients, introducing soil microbes, increasing water retention and improving drainage. Compost can be purchased or you can make it in your own backyard.

Microclimates are small areas that are generally warmer or colder than the surrounding area. Buildings, fences, trees and other large structures can provide extra shelter in winter, but may trap heat in summer, thus creating a warmer microclimate. The bottoms of hills are usually colder than the tops, but may not be as windy. Take advantage of these areas when you plan your garden and choose your

Hardiness Zones Map

TEMPERATURE (˚C)	ZONE	TEMPERATURE (˚F)
–28.9 to –31.6	4b	–20 to –25
–26.2 to –28.8	5a	–15 to –20
–23.4 to –26.1	5b	–10 to –15
–20.6 to –23.3	6a	–5 to –10
–17.8 to –20.5	6b	0 to –5
–15.1 to 17.7	7a	5 to 0
–12.3 to 15.0	7b	10 to 5
–9.5 to –12.2	8a	15 to 10
–6.7 to–9.4	8b	20 to 15
–3.9 to –6.6	9a	25 to 20
–1.2 to –3.8	9b	30 to 25

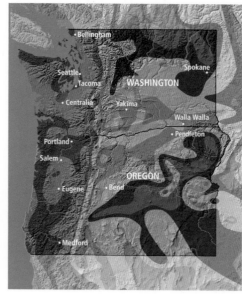

plants; you may even grow out-of-zone plants successfully in a warm, sheltered location.

Selecting Plants

It's important to purchase healthy plants that are free of pests and diseases. Such plants will establish quickly in your garden and won't introduce problems that may spread to other plants. You should have a good idea of what the plant is supposed to look like—the color and shape of the leaves and the habit of the plant—and then inspect the plant for signs of disease or infestation.

The majority of plants are container grown. This is an efficient way for nurseries and greenhouses to grow plants, but when plants grow in a restricted space for too long, they can become pot bound, with their roots densely encircling the inside of the pot. Avoid purchasing plants in this condition; they are often stressed and take longer to establish. Sometimes they may not establish at all. It is often possible to remove pots temporarily to look at the condition of the roots. Check for soil-borne insects and rotten roots at the same time.

Planting Basics

The following tips apply to all plants:
• Prepare the garden before planting. Dig over the soil, pull up any weeds and make any needed amendments before you begin planting, if possible. This may be more difficult in established beds to which you want to add a single plant. The prepared area should be at least twice the size of the plant you want to put in, and preferably the expected size of the mature plant.
• Settle the soil with water. Good contact between the roots and the soil is important, but if you press the soil down too firmly, as often happens when you step on the soil, you can cause compaction, which reduces the movement of water through the soil and leaves very few air spaces. Instead, pour water in as you fill the hole with soil. The water will settle the soil evenly without allowing it to compact.
• Unwrap the roots. Remove any container before planting to give roots the chance to spread out naturally when planted. In particular, you should remove plastic containers, fiber pots, wire and burlap before planting trees. Fiber pots decompose very slowly, if at all, and wick moisture away from the plant. Synthetic burlap won't decompose, and wire can strangle the roots as they mature. The only exceptions to this rule are peat pots and pellets used to start annuals and vegetables; these decompose and can be planted with the young transplants.
• Accommodate the rootball. If you prepared your planting spot ahead of time, your planting hole will only need to be big enough to accommodate the rootball with the roots spread out slightly.
• Know the mature size. Plant based on how big the plants will grow rather than how big they are when you plant them. Large plants should have enough room to

1. Gently remove container.

2. Ensure proper planting depth.

3. Backfill with amended soil.

mature without interfering with walls, roof overhangs, power lines and walkways.

- Plant at the same depth. Plants generally like to grow at a certain level in relation to the soil and should be planted at the same level they were growing at before you transplanted them.
- Identify your plants. Keep track of what's what in your garden by putting a tag next to your plant when you plant it, or by making a drawing with plant names and locations. It is very easy for beginning gardeners to forget exactly what they planted and where they planted it.
- Water deeply and infrequently. It's better to water deeply once every week or two rather than to water a little bit more often. This forces roots to grow as they search for water and helps them survive dry spells when water bans may restrict your watering regime. Always check the rootzone before you water. More gardeners overwater than underwater.

Annuals and perennials in a mixed border

Annuals

Annuals are planted new each year and are only expected to last for a single growing season. Their flowers and decorative foliage provide bright splashes of color and can fill in spaces around immature trees, shrubs and perennials.

Annuals are easy to plant and are usually sold in small packs of four or six. The roots quickly fill the space in these small packs, so the small rootball should be broken up before planting. Split the ball in two up the center or run your thumb up each side to break up the roots.

Many annuals are grown from seed and can be started directly in the garden. Consult an annual book such as Lone Pine's *Annuals for Washington and Oregon* for further information on the care and growing of annuals.

Perennials

Perennials grow for three or more years. They usually die back to the ground each fall and send up new shoots in spring, though some are evergreen. They often have a shorter bloom period than annuals, but require less care.

Many perennials benefit from being divided every few years. This keeps them growing and blooming vigorously, and in

4. Settle backfilled soil with water.

5. Water the plant well.

6. Add a layer of mulch.

some cases controls their spread. Dividing involves digging the plant up, removing dead bits, breaking the plant into several pieces and replanting some or all pieces. Extra pieces can be given as gifts to family, friends and neighbors. Consult a perennial book such as Lone Pine's *Perennials for Washington and Oregon* for further information on the care of perennials.

Trees & Shrubs

Trees and shrubs provide the bones of the garden. They are often the slowest-growing plants, but usually live the longest. Characterized by leaf type, they may be deciduous or evergreen, and needled or broad-leaved.

Trees should have as little disturbed soil as possible at the bottom of the planting hole. Loose dirt settles over time and sinking even an inch can kill some trees.

Staking is only necessary for newly planted trees over 5' (1.5 m) tall. Pruning is more often required for shrubs than trees. It helps them maintain an attractive shape and can improve blooming. Consult Lone Pine's *Tree and Shrub Gardening for Washington and Oregon* for information about pruning trees and shrubs.

Roses are lovely on their own or in mixed borders.

Roses

Roses are beautiful shrubs with lovely, often fragrant blooms. Traditionally, most roses only bloomed once in the growing season, but new varieties bloom all, or almost all, summer.

Generally, roses prefer a fertile, well-prepared planting area. A rule of thumb is to prepare an area 24" (60 cm) across, front to back and side to side, and 24" (60 cm) deep. Add plenty of compost or other fertile organic matter and keep roses well watered during the growing season. Many roses are quite durable and will adapt to poorer conditions.

Roses, like all shrubs, have specific pruning requirements. A book such as Lone Pine's *Roses for Washington and Oregon* will provide detailed information.

Trees and shrubs provide backbone to the mixed border.

Climbing hydrangea sets off a brick wall nicely.

Rosemary is a wonderful herb for growing in pots.

Vines

Vines or climbing plants are useful for screening and shade, especially in a location too small for a tree. They may be woody or herbaceous and annual or perennial.

Most vines need sturdy supports to grow up on. Trellises, arbors, porch railings, fences, walls, poles and trees are all possible supports. If a support is needed, ensure it's in place before you plant to avoid disturbing the roots later.

Lilies bloom throughout the summer.

Bulbs

The bulb section of this book includes some plants that grow from corms and tubers. All of these plants have fleshy underground storage organs that allow them to survive extended periods of dormancy. They are often grown for the bright splashes of color their flowers provide. They may be spring, summer or fall flowering.

Hardy bulbs can be left in the ground and will flower every year, but many popular tender plants grow from bulbs, corms or tubers. These tender plants are generally lifted from the garden in fall as the foliage dies back. Store them in a cool, frost-free location for winter and replant in spring.

Herbs

Herbs may be medicinal or culinary and often both. A few common culinary herbs are listed in this book. Even if you don't cook with them, the often-fragrant foliage adds its aroma to the garden and the plants have decorative forms, leaves and flowers.

Many herbs have pollen-producing flowers that attract butterflies, bees and hummingbirds to the garden. They also attract predatory insects. These useful insects help to manage your pest problems by feasting on insects such as aphids, mealy bugs and whiteflies.

Ornamental grasses, ferns and other foliage plants

Foliage is an important consideration when choosing plants for your garden. Although many plants look spectacular in bloom, they can seem rather dull without flowers. Including a variety of plants with unique, interesting, or striking foliage in your garden can provide all the color and texture you want without the need to rely on flowers.

Ornamental grasses are gaining popularity. Grasses offer a variety of textures and foliage colors, and at least three seasons of interest. Some grasses will thrive in any garden condition, including hot and dry to cool and wet temperatures, and in all types of soils.

Ornamental grasses have very few insect or disease problems. They require very little maintenance other than cutting the perennial grasses back in fall or spring. If you plan to leave dried grass standing for winter interest, be aware that it can present a fire hazard. Dry grass is highly flammable and should be cut back in fall if it is near a house or other structure.

Ferns are ancient plants that have adapted to many environments. The fern family is a very large group of plants with interesting foliage in a wide array of shapes and colors. Ferns do not produce flowers, but reproduce by spores borne in interesting structures on the undersides and margins of the foliage. Ferns are generally planted in moist, shaded gardens, but some will thrive in dry shade under dense evergreens.

We included some grass-like foliage plants in this book. Sedge, rush and phormium can be used with or as substitutes for ornamental grasses. We also added a variety of plants grown for foliage throughout the book. Many annuals, perennials, trees, shrubs, vines and herbs have wonderful foliage, and will be an asset to your garden landscape.

A Final Comment

Don't be afraid to experiment. No matter how many books you read, trying things yourself is the best way to learn and to find out what will grow in your garden. Use the information as guidelines, and have fun!

Ornamental grasses add color, variety and texture.

African Daisy
Osteospermum

*A*frican daisies are colorful, care-free plants that retain their good looks late into fall and can withstand temperatures as low as 25° F (−4° C). New varieties have better heat and moisture tolerance.

Growing

Plant in **full sun,** in **light, evenly moist, moderately fertile, well-drained** soil when the soil warms in spring. Do not overwater or let the plants wilt; use organic mulch to cut down on watering. Deadhead to encourage new growth and more flowers. Pinch young plants to encourage a bushier form.

Tips

African daisies work well in containers or beds. Their flowers look great mixed with plants like petunias or verbenas.

Recommended

O. ecklonis grows upright to almost prostrate, but it is often rejected in favor of its wonderful cultivars. **Passion Mix** has free-flowering, heat-tolerant plants. The **Springstar Series** boasts compact, early-flowering plants. **Starwhirls Series** flowers have unique spoon-shaped petals.

Proven Winners' *O.* **Symphony Series** has mounding plants. They tolerate heat well and flower through the summer.

Starwhirls Series (above), *O. ecklonis* (below)

You may find African daisy listed as either Dimorphotheca *or* Osteospermum. Dimorphotheca *is a closely related genus that formerly included all the plants now listed as* Osteospermum.

Also called: Cape daisy **Features:** colorful flowers, easy care, heat tolerance
Flower color: white, peach, orange, yellow, pink, lavender, purple; often with dark centers of blue-purple or other colors
Height: 12–20" (30–50 cm)
Spread: 10–20" (25–50 cm)

Bachelor's Buttons
Centaurea

Bachelor's buttons is an old-time favorite, and it remains a popular and highly desirable annual today. In a garden with poor, rocky or sandy soil, pair this tough and hard-to-kill plant with California poppies for a bright, summer display.

Growing
Bachelor's buttons grow best in **full sun**. **Average to fertile, moist, well-drained** soil is preferable, but it will tolerate any soil, including poor and dry soil. Light frost won't harm the plants.

The long-lived cut flowers can be pinned to lapels or poked through buttonholes.

Seed started indoors should be planted in peat pots or pellets to avoid disturbing roots during transplanting. Plant out around the last frost. Shear spent flowers and old foliage in mid-summer for fresh new growth. Deadheading will prolong blooming.

Tips
Bachelor's buttons is useful in a mixed border, wildflower bed or cottage-style garden. It looks great when massed, works well in containers and makes a wonderful cut flower.

Recommended
C. cyanus is an upright annual that self-seeds year after year. Many cultivars are available.

Also called: cornflower **Features:** bright flowers, tough and self-seeding plant
Flower color: mostly blue, with shades of red, pink, white and purple **Height:** 8–32" (20–80 cm)
Spread: 6–24" (15–60 cm)

Bacopa
Sutera

Bacopa snuggles under and around the stems of taller plants, forming a dense carpet dotted with tiny, white to pale lavender flowers, and eventually drifting over pot edges to form a waterfall of stars.

Growing
Bacopa grows well in **full sun to partial shade**, with protection from the hot afternoon sun. The soil should be of **average fertility, humus rich, moist** and **well drained**.

If this plant to dries out, its leaves will quickly die. Cutting back dead growth may encourage new shoots to form.

Tips
Bacopa is a popular plant for hanging baskets, mixed containers and window boxes. It forms an attractive, spreading mound in a rock garden, but it will need regular watering.

Recommended
S. cordata is a compact, trailing plant that bears small, white flowers all summer. Cultivars with larger white flowers, lavender flowers or gold and green variegated foliage are available.

Bacopa is a perennial that is grown as an annual outdoors. It will thrive as a houseplant in a bright room.

Features: decorative flowers, foliage, habit **Flower color:** white, lavender **Height:** 3–5" (8–13 cm) **Spread:** 12–20" (30–50 cm)

Begonia
Begonia

Whether you want beautiful flowers, a compact habit or decorative foliage, there is a begonia to fulfill your shade gardening needs.

Growing
Begonias prefer **light to partial shade** and **fertile, neutral to acidic, well-drained** soil with **lots of organic matter**. Some wax begonias tolerate sun if their soil is kept moist. Allow the soil to dry out slightly between waterings, particularly for tuberous begonias. Plant begonias only in warm soil. In cold soil, they may become stunted and fail to thrive.

Tips
Plant trailing tuberous begonias in hanging baskets and along rock walls. Wax begonias make attractive edging plants. Rex begonias are useful as specimen plants in containers and beds.

Recommended
B. Rex Cultorum Hybrids (rex begonias) are grown for their dramatic, colorful foliage.

B. semperflorens (wax begonias) have a neat, rounded habit, pink, white, red or bicolored flowers and green, bronze, reddish or white-variegated foliage.

B. x tuberhybrida (tuberous begonias) are generally sold as tubers. Their flowers bloom in many shades of red, pink, yellow, orange or white.

Tuberous begonia (above & below)

Water along the edge of containers or around the dripline of in-ground tuberous begonias to prevent tuber rot—never water near the stem. Keep the mildew-prone foliage dry.

Photos: tuberous begonia **Features:** colorful flowers, decorative foliage **Flower color:** pink, white, red, yellow, orange, bicolored or picotee **Height:** 6–24" (15–60 cm) **Spread:** 6–24" (15–60 cm)

Calendula

Calendula

'Apricot Surprise' (above), *C. officinalis* (below)

Calendulas are bright and charming. They produce attractive flowers in warm colors all summer and fall.

Growing

Calendula does equally well in **full sun** or **partial shade** in **well-drained** soil of **average fertility**. It likes cool weather and can withstand a light frost. Deadhead to prolong blooming and keep plants looking neat.

Young plants are sometimes difficult to find in nurseries. Sow seed directly into the garden in mid-spring. A second sowing in early summer ensures a good fall display.

Tips

This informal plant looks attractive in borders and mixed into the vegetable garden. It can also be used in mixed planters. Calendula is a cold-hardy annual and often continues flowering, even through a layer of snow, until the ground freezes completely.

Recommended

C. officinalis is a vigorous, tough, upright plant that bears daisy-like, single or double flowers in a wide range of yellow and orange shades. Several cultivars are available.

Calendula flowers are popular kitchen herbs that can be added to stews for color or to salads for flavoring. They can also be brewed into an infusion that is useful as a wash for minor cuts and bruises.

Also called: pot marigold, English marigold
Features: colorful flowers, long blooming period
Flower color: cream, yellow, gold, orange, apricot **Height:** 12–30" (30–75 cm)
Spread: 12–18" (30–45 cm)

California Poppy
Eschscholzia

California poppies cheerfully reseed themselves year after year. They look great in meadow or rock gardens, or popping up through cracks of a flagstone path.

Growing

California poppy prefers **full sun** and **well-drained** soil of **poor to average fertility**. In rich soil, the plant will grow lush and green, but will bear few, if any, flowers. This plant is drought tolerant once established, but it requires lots of water for germination and until it begins flowering.

The petals of California poppy can be eaten. They have little nutritional value but the color will brighten up a salad.

Never start this plant indoors because it dislikes having its roots disturbed. California poppy will sprout quickly when sown directly in the garden in early to mid-spring. In mild areas, seeds sown in early fall will produce blooms in spring.

Tips

California poppy can be included in an annual border or annual planting in a cottage garden.

Recommended

E. californica forms a mound of delicate, feathery, blue-green foliage. It bears satiny flowers all summer. Cultivars with semi-double or double flowers and flowers in red, cream or pink are available.

Features: colorful flowers; attractive, feathery foliage **Flower color:** orange, yellow or red; less commonly pink, violet or cream
Height: 30–60 cm (12–24")
Spread: 15–30 cm (6–12")

China Aster
Callistephus

China aster's vivid and dense flowers will steal the spotlight in your garden all summer long, provided you feed and water them adequately.

Growing

China aster prefers **full sun** but tolerates partial shade. The soil should be **fertile, evenly moist** and **well drained**. A **neutral or alkaline** pH is preferable. If your garden has acidic soil, grow smaller China aster varieties in pots or planters, where the soil pH can be adjusted.

Plant out once the soil has warmed. This plant doesn't like having its roots disturbed, so start seeds in peat pots or peat pellets. China aster has a shallow root system that can dry out quickly; mulch to conserve moisture.

Tips

Use smaller varieties as edging and taller varieties for cut flowers and at the back of the border. Tall varieties may require staking.

Recommended

C. chinensis is the source of many varieties and cultivars, which come in three height groups: dwarf, medium and tall.

China asters are heavy feeders, so you will need to fertilize them regularly to produce flowers like those in the catalogs.

Features: colorful flowers of varying shapes and sizes **Flower color:** purple, blue, pink, red, white, peach, yellow **Height:** 12–36" (30–90 cm) **Spread:** 10–18" (25–45 cm)

Coleus
Solenostemon (Coleus)

Try taking coleus cuttings from a mother plant and overwintering them inside. The cuttings root easily in a glass of water.

There is a coleus for everyone. This plant has almost limitless colors, textures and variations.

Growing
Coleus prefers **light shade** or **partial shade** but tolerates full shade if isn't too dense and full sun if the plants are watered regularly. The soil should be **average to fertile, humus rich, moist** and **well drained**.

Place the seeds in a refrigerator for one or two days before planting them on the soil surface; the cold temperatures help the seeds break dormancy. They need light to germinate. Seedlings will be green at first, but leaf variegation will develop as the plants mature.

Tips
Coleus looks dramatic grouped in beds, borders and mixed containers, or planted as edging.

Pinch off flower buds once they have developed. Coleus flowers tend to stretch out and become less attractive after they bloom.

Recommended
S. scutellarioides (*Coleus blumei* var. *verschaffeltii*) forms a bushy mound of multi-colored, slightly toothed to very ruffled foliage. Dozens of cultivars are available, but many cannot be started from seed. New varieties that tolerate full sun and have larger, more colorful foliage are available.

Features: brightly colored foliage
Flower color: light purple, grown as a foliage plant **Height:** 6–36" (15–90 cm)
Spread: usually equal to height

Cosmos
Cosmos

Annual cosmos (above & below)

Cosmos are low-cost, low-maintenance, cottage garden flowers that are easy to grow and never fail to delight.

Growing

Cosmos like **full sun** and **well-drained** soil with **poor to average fertility**. Plant them after the last frost. Overfertilizing and overwatering can reduce the number of flowers; cut faded blooms to encourage more buds. These plants often self-seed.

Tips

Cosmos look attractive in cottage gardens, at the back of a border or mass planted in an informal bed.

To avoid staking, plant cosmos against a fence or in a sheltered location, or grow its shorter varieties. To stake plants, push twiggy branches into the ground when the plants are young and allow them to grow up between the branches. The mature plant will hide the branches.

Recommended

C. bipinnatus (annual cosmos) is an erect plant with fine, fern-like foliage. It and its many cultivars bear magenta, rose, pink, white and bicolored flowers, usually with yellow centers.

C. sulphureus (yellow cosmos) is a smaller, denser plant than *C. bipinnatus*, and has gold, orange, scarlet and yellow flowers. Sow this plant directly in the garden.

Features: colorful flowers, fern-like foliage, easy to grow **Flower color:** magenta, rose, pink, purple, white, yellow, orange, scarlet **Height:** 12"–7' (30 cm–2.1 m) **Spread:** 12–18" (30–45 cm)

Dusty Miller
Senecio

Dusty miller makes an artful addition to planters, window boxes and mixed borders where the soft, silvery gray, deeply lobed foliage makes a good backdrop for the brightly colored flowers of other annuals.

Growing
Dusty miller prefers **full sun** but tolerates light shade. The soil should be of **average fertility** and **well drained**.

Tips
This plant's soft, silvery, lacy foliage is its main feature. Dusty miller is used

primarily as an edging plant, but also in beds, borders and containers.

Pinch off the flowers before they bloom. They aren't showy and they steal energy that would otherwise go to producing more foliage.

Dusty miller performs best as an annual. If it does survive the winter, its silver leaves will look weary and tarnished. Cut them back hard in May to encourage fresh growth.

Recommended
S. cineraria forms a mound of fuzzy, silvery gray, lobed or finely divided foliage. Many cultivars with impressive foliage colors and shapes have been developed.

Features: silvery foliage, neat habit **Flower color:** yellow to cream, grown for silvery foliage **Height:** 12–24" (30–60 cm) **Spread:** equal to height or slightly narrower

Dwarf Morning Glory

Convolvulus

This well-mannered, relatively pest-free plant is easy to care for. It's a great addition to a new garden because it doesn't need fertile or well-worked soil, and it adapts to poor growing conditions.

Growing

Dwarf morning glories prefer **full sun**. The soil should be of **poor** or **average fertility** and **well drained**. These plants may not flower well in rich, moist soil. Sow seeds or plant in mid- to late spring.

Soak the seeds in water overnight before planting them. If starting seeds early indoors, use peat pots to avoid root damage when transplanting.

Tips

Plant these compact, mounding plants in containers, hanging baskets, rock walls and borders.

Recommended

C. tricolor bears flowers that last only a single day, blooming in the morning and twisting shut that evening. Several cultivars are available.

This annual is related to the dreaded bindweeds (C. arvensis *and* C. sepium*), but it doesn't share its weedy cousins' unstoppable twining and spreading power.*

Features: richly colored flowers, easy care
Flower color: blue, purple, pink **Height:** 12–16"
(30–40 cm) **Spread:** 9–12" (23–30 cm)

Fan Flower

Scaevola

Given the right conditions, this Australian plant will flower profusely from April through to frost.

Fan flower's intriguing one-sided flowers add interest to hanging baskets, planters and window boxes.

Growing

Fan flower grows well in **full sun** or **light shade**. The soil should be of **average fertility, moist** and **very well drained**. Water regularly because this plant doesn't like to dry out completely. It does, however, recover quickly from wilting when watered.

Tips

Fan flower is a popular choice for hanging baskets and containers, but it can also be used along the tops of rock walls and in rock gardens where it will trail down. This plant makes an interesting addition to mixed borders and it can be planted under shrubs, where the long, trailing stems will form an attractive groundcover.

Fan flower responds well to pinching and trimming. Frequently pinching the tips or trimming the entire plant back will keep it bushy and blooming.

Recommended

S. aemula forms a mound of foliage from which trailing stems emerge. The fan-shaped flowers come in shades of purple, usually with white bases. The species is rarely grown because there are many improved cultivars.

Features: unique flowers, trailing habit
Flower color: blue, purple **Height:** up to 8" (20 cm) **Spread:** up to 4' (1.2 m)

Fuchsia

Fuchsia

These beautiful, shade-blooming plants should be grown in every garden. Cool summer climates are perfect for growing fuchsias.

Growing

Fuchsias grow in **partial** or **light shade**. They will not tolerate summer heat, and full sun can be too hot for them. Soil should be **fertile, moist** and **well drained**. Plant them after the last frost.

Fuchsias should be deadheaded. Pluck the swollen seedpods from behind the fading petals or the seeds will ripen and rob the plant of energy it needs for flower production.

Fuchsias bloom on new growth and prefer a plant food high in nitrogen that encourages new growth.

Tips

Plant upright fuchsias in mixed planters, beds and borders. Pendulous fuchsias are most often used in hanging baskets, but they make attractive additions to planters and rock gardens.

F. x hybrida (above & below)

Recommended

F. Angel's Earrings Series from Proven Winners tolerate heat and humidity.

Dozens of cultivars of **F. x *hybrida*** are available in both upright and pendulous forms. Cultivars with bronzy red foliage are also available.

Some gardeners who have grown fuchsias over several years have trained the plants to adopt tree forms.

Features: colorful, pendent flowers **Flower color:** pink, red, orange, purple, purple-blue or white; often bicolored **Height:** 6–36" (15–90 cm) **Spread:** 8–36" (20–90 cm)

Geranium

Pelargonium

Zonal geranium (above), Martha Washington geranium (below)

Tough, predictable, sun-loving and drought-resistant, geraniums have earned their respected place in the annual garden. For something out of the ordinary, seek out the scented geraniums with their fragrant and often decorative foliage.

Growing

Geraniums prefer **full sun** but will tolerate partial shade, though they may not bloom as profusely in shade. The soil should be **fertile** and **well drained**.

Deadheading is essential to keep geraniums blooming and looking neat.

Tips

Geraniums are very popular annual plants, used in borders, beds, planters, hanging baskets and window boxes.

Recommended

P. domesticum (Martha Washington geranium) has heart-shaped foliage and larger, frillier flowers than other geraniums. It works well in containers but does not tolerate heat as well as do other varieties.

P. peltatum (ivy-leaved geranium) has thick, waxy leaves and a trailing habit. Ivy-leaved geranium is one of the best plants to include in a mixed hanging basket.

P. zonale (zonal geranium) is a bushy plant with red, pink, purple, orange or white flowers and, frequently, banded or multi-colored foliage.

P. species and **cultivars** (scented geraniums, scented pelargoniums) are geraniums with scented foliage. The scents are grouped into the categories of rose, mint, citrus, fruit, spice and pungent.

Features: colorful flowers, decorative or scented foliage, variable habits **Flower color:** red, pink, violet, orange, salmon, white or purple **Height:** 8–24" (20–60 cm) **Spread:** 6"–4' (15 cm–1.2 m)

Impatiens
Impatiens

New Guinea hybrid (above), Busy Lizzie (below)

Impatiens are the high-wattage darlings of the shade garden, delivering masses of colorful flowers.

Growing

Impatiens do best in **partial shade** or **light shade** but tolerate full shade or, if kept moist, full sun. New Guinea and balsam impatiens grow well in sunny locations. The soil should be **fertile, humus rich, moist** and **well drained**.

Tips

Impatiens are known for their ability to grow and flower profusely even in shade. Mass plant them in beds under trees, along shady fences or walls or in porch planters. They look lovely in hanging baskets.

Recommended

I. balsamina (balsam impatiens) are upright plants that bloom in shades of purple, red, pink or white. Several double-flowered cultivars exist.

I. hawkeri (New Guinea hybrids; New Guinea impatiens) flowers in shades of red, orange, pink, purple or white. The foliage is often variegated with a yellow stripe down the center of each leaf.

I. walleriana (busy Lizzie) flowers in shades of purple, red, burgundy, pink, yellow, salmon, orange, apricot and white, and it can be bi-colored. Dozens of cultivars are available.

Features: colorful flowers, grows well in shade
Flower color: shades of purple, red, burgundy, pink, yellow, salmon, orange, apricot, white; also bicolored **Height:** 6–36" (15–90 cm)
Spread: 12–24" (30–60 cm)

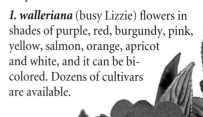

Licorice Plant

Helichrysum

'Silver' (above), 'Limelight' (below)

This tough plant can handle frosty weather, rain storms, heat waves, browsing deer and pesky slugs. It's a perfect choice for carefree gardeners.

Growing

Licorice plant prefers **full sun**. The soil should be of **poor to average fertility, neutral** or **alkaline** and **well drained**. Licorice plant wilts when the soil dries but revives quickly once watered. If it outgrows its space, snip it back with a pair of pruners, shears or even scissors.

Tips

Licorice plant is a perennial grown as an annual, and it is prized for its foliage rather than its flowers. Include it in your hanging baskets, planters and window boxes to provide a soft, silvery backdrop to the colorful flowers of other plants. Licorice plant can also be used as a groundcover in beds, borders, rock gardens and along the tops of retaining walls.

Recommended

H. petiolare is a trailing plant with fuzzy, gray-green leaves. Cultivars are more common than the species and include varieties with lime green, silver or variegated leaves.

Features: trailing habit; colorful, fuzzy foliage
Flower color: plant grown for foliage
Height: 20" (50 cm) **Spread:** about 3' (90 cm); sometimes up to 6' (1.8 m)

Lobelia
Lobelia

Lobelia is a lovely plant that adds color to shady spots and blends well with fuchsias and begonias. Luckily, lobelia also does well in the sun. Lobelias and marigolds make a striking combination.

Growing
Lobelia grows well in **full sun** or **partial shade**, in **fertile, moist, fairly well-drained** soil high in **organic matter**. Lobelia likes cool summer nights. Ensure that its soil stays moist in hot weather. Plant out after the last frost.

Because seedlings are prone to damping off, be sure to use good, clean, seed-starting soil mix. Damping off causes plants to rot at the soil level, flop over and die.

Tips
Use lobelia along the edges of beds and borders, on rock walls, in rock gardens, mixed containers and hanging baskets.

Trim lobelia back after its first wave of flowers. This helps ensure the plant flowers through summer. In hot areas, it may die back over summer but usually revives as the weather cools.

Recommended
L. erinus may be rounded and bushy or low and trailing. Many cultivars are available in both forms.

'Sapphire' (above), 'Cascade Series' (below)

These lovely plants from the bellflower family contain deadly alkaloids and have poisoned people who tried to use them as herbal medicine.

Features: abundant, colorful flowers
Flower color: purple, blue, pink, white or red **Height:** 3–9" (8–23 cm) **Spread:** 6" (15 cm) or wider

Mallow

Lavatera

L. trimestris (above), *L. cachemiriana* (below)

Mallows are great plants for tough growing conditions. Many flowers fail in dry, infertile soil, but mallow just keeps blooming and only stops with the first hard frost of fall.

Growing

Mallow prefers **full sun**. The soil should be of **average fertility, light** and **well drained**. This plant likes cool, moist weather and shelter from the wind. Use peat pots when starting seeds indoors. Mallow resents having its roots disturbed. Direct seeding is best. Plant out after last frost.

Stake tall varieties to keep them from falling over in summer rain.

Tips

These large, shrubby plants work well in beds and borders or behind smaller plants for a colorful backdrop. Or try planting them as a temporary hedge. The flowers can be used for cutting and are edible.

Recommended

L. arborea (tree mallow) is a large plant with funnel-shaped, pinkish purple flowers.

L. cachemiriana is another large plant that bears light pink flowers.

L. trimestris is a bushy plant that bears red, pink, rose pink, salmon pink or white funnel-shaped flowers.

Features: delicate flowers, easy care, tough plant **Flower color:** rose, pink, salmon or white **Height:** 24"–4' (60 cm–1.2 m) **Spread:** 18–24" (45–60 cm)

Marigold

Tagetes

From the large, exotic, ruffled flowers of African marigold to the tiny flowers on the low-growing signet marigold, the warm colors and fresh scent of marigolds add a festive air to the garden.

Growing

Marigolds grow best in **full sun**. The soil should be of **average fertility** and **well drained**. These plants are drought tolerant and hold up well in windy, rainy weather. However, too much water may cause rot. Minimize overhead watering. Sow seed directly in the garden after the chance of frost has passed. Deadhead to prolong blooming and to keep plants tidy.

Tips

Mass planted or mixed with other plants, marigolds make a vibrant addition to beds, borders and container gardens. These plants will thrive in the hottest, driest parts of your garden.

Recommended

T. erecta (African marigold, American marigold, Aztec marigold) are the largest plants with the biggest flowers.

T. patula (French marigold) is low growing and has a wide range of flower colors.

T. tenuifolia (signet marigold) has feathery foliage and small, dainty flowers.

T. **Triploid Hybrids** have huge flowers and compact growth.

African marigold mixed border (above), French marigold (below)

Slugs really enjoy the marigold's scented foliage—be sure to protect your plants from these creatures.

Features: brightly colored flowers, fragrant foliage, easy to grow **Flower color:** yellow, red, orange, brown, gold, cream, bicolored **Height:** 6–36" (15–90 cm) **Spread:** 12–24" (30–60 cm)

Million Bells

Calibrachoa

Million bells is charming, and given the right conditions, it will bloom continually throughout the growing season.

Growing

Million bells prefers **full sun**. The soil should be **fertile, moist** and **well drained**. Although it prefers to be watered regularly, million bells is fairly drought resistant once established. The flowers develop hardiness as the weather cools, enabling them to bloom well into autumn. Million bells can survive temperatures as low as 20° F (–7° C).

Tips

A popular choice for planters and hanging baskets, million bells also looks attractive in beds and borders. It grows all summer and needs plenty of room to spread or it will overtake other flowers. Pinch back to keep plants compact. To protect the flower petals from rain, place hanging baskets under the eaves of the house or porch.

Recommended

Calibrachoa **Hybrids** have a dense, trailing habit, and they bear small flowers that look like petunias. Cultivars are available in a wide range of flower colors, including striking bicolored varieties. The peachy **'Terracotta'** looks great paired with intensely colored foliage plants in clay pots.

'Trailing Blue' (above), 'Trailing Pink' (below)

Million bells flowers close at night and on cloudy days.

Also called: calibrachoa, trailing petunia
Features: colorful flowers, trailing habit
Flower color: pink, purple, yellow, red-orange, white, blue **Height:** 6–12"
(15–30 cm) **Spread:** Up to 24" (60 cm)

Moss Rose
Portulaca

For a brilliant show in the hottest, driest, most neglected area of the garden, you can't go wrong with moss rose.

Growing

Moss rose requires **full sun**. The soil should be of **poor fertility, sandy** and **well drained**. To ensure that you will have plants where you want them, start seed indoors. If you sow directly outdoors, the tiny seeds may get washed away by rain and the plants will pop up in unexpected places.

Tips

Moss rose will grow well under the eaves of a house or in a dry, rocky, exposed area. It also makes a great addition to a hanging basket on a sunny front porch. Remember to water it occasionally. As long as the location is sunny, this plant will do well with minimal care.

Recommended

P. grandiflora forms a bushy mound of succulent foliage. It bears delicate, papery, rose-like flowers profusely all summer. Many cultivars are available, including those with flowers that stay open on cloudy days.

These plants can be placed close together and allowed to intertwine for an interesting and attractive effect.

Also called: portulaca
Features: colorful, drought-resistant summer flowers **Flower color:** red, pink, yellow, white, purple, orange, peach **Height:** 4–8" (10–20 cm)
Spread: 6–12" (15–30 cm) or wider

Nasturtium
Tropaeolum

'Alaska' (above), *T. majus* (below)

Combine nasturtiums with vegetables and other ornamental edible plants in containers and window boxes. The leaves and flowers are edible, and add a peppery flavor to salads.

These fast-growing, brightly colored flowers are easy to grow, making them popular with beginners and experienced gardeners.

Growing
Nasturtiums prefer **full sun** but tolerate some shade. The soil should be of **poor to average fertility, light, moist** and **well drained**. Plants grown in fertile soil will produce many leaves and few flowers. Let the soil drain completely between waterings. Set out plants or sow directly in the garden once the danger of frost has passed.

Tips
Nasturtiums are used in beds, borders, containers and hanging baskets. The climbing varieties are grown up trellises or over rock walls or places that need concealing. These plants thrive in poor locations, and they make an interesting addition to hard-to-mow slopes.

Recommended
T. majus has a trailing habit, but many of the cultivars have bushier, more refined habits. Cultivars are available in a range of flower colors and with variegated foliage.

Features: brightly colored flowers, attractive leaves, edible leaves and flowers, varied habits **Flower color:** red, orange, yellow, burgundy, pink, cream, gold, white or bi-colored **Height:** 12–18" (30–45 cm) for dwarf varieties; up to 10' (3 m) for trailing varieties **Spread:** equal to height

Petunia

Petunia

'Blue Wave' (above), multiflora petunias (above & below)

For speedy growth, prolific blooming and ease of care, petunias are hard to beat. Even the most neglected plants will continue to bloom all summer.

Growing

Petunias prefer **full sun**. The soil should be of **average fertility, light, sandy** and **well drained**. In mid-summer, pinch the plant back halfway or cut the blooms for arrangements. This will keep the plant compact and bushy, and will encourage new growth and flowers.

When sowing, press seeds into soil surface but don't cover them with soil.

Tips

Use petunias in beds, borders, containers and hanging baskets.

Recommended

P. x *hybrida* is a large group of popular annuals that fall into three categories. **Grandifloras** have the largest flowers in the widest range of colors, but they can be damaged by rain. **Multifloras** bear more flowers that are smaller and less easily damaged by heavy rain. **Millifloras** have the smallest flowers in the narrowest range of colors, but they are the most prolific bloomers and the least likely to suffer rain damage.

Some varieties, especially those with purple or white flowers, are very fragrant.

Features: colorful flowers, versatile plants
Flower color: pink, purple, red, white, yellow, coral, blue or bicolored **Height:** 6–18" (15–45 cm)
Spread: 12–24" (30–60 cm) or wider

Salvia
Salvia

Scarlet sage (above), mealy cup sage (below)

The genus name Salvia comes from the Latin salvus, 'to save,' which refers to the medicinal properties of several species.

Salvias should have a place in every annual garden. There are over 900 species of *Salvia*, and the attractive and varied forms have something to offer every garden style.

Growing
All salvia plants prefer **full sun** but will tolerate light shade. The soil should be **moist, well drained** and of **average to rich fertility** with lots of **organic matter** mixed in.

Tips
Salvias look good grouped in beds and borders and in containers. The long-lasting cut flowers are good for arrangements.

To keep plants producing flowers, water often and fertilize monthly.

Recommended
S. coccinea (Texas sage) is a bushy, upright plant that bears whorled spikes of white, pink, blue or purple flowers.

S. farinacea (mealy cup sage, blue sage) has bright blue flowers clustered along stems powdered with silver. Cultivars are available.

S. splendens (salvia, scarlet sage) is grown for its spikes of bright red, tubular flowers. Recently, cultivars have become available in white, pink, purple and orange.

S. viridis (*S. horminium*; annual clary sage) is grown for its colorful pink, purple, blue or white bracts, not its flowers.

Also called: sage **Features:** colorful summer flowers, attractive foliage **Flower color:** red, blue, purple, burgundy, pink, orange, salmon, yellow, cream, white or bicolored
Height: 8–36" (20–90 cm) **Spread:** 8–16" (20–40 cm)

Snapdragon
Antirrhinum

Snapdragons are among the most appealing plants. The flower colors are always rich and vibrant, and even the most jaded gardeners are tempted to squeeze open the dragons' mouths.

Growing

Snapdragons prefer **full sun** but tolerate light or partial shade. The soil should be **fertile, rich in organic matter, neutral to alkaline** and **well drained**. These plants do not perform well in acidic soil. Do not cover seeds when sowing because they require light for germination.

To encourage bushy growth, pinch the tips of the young plants. Cut off the flower spikes as they fade to promote further blooming and to prevent the plant from dying back before the end of the season.

Tips

The height of the variety dictates the best place for it in a border—the shortest varieties work well near the front, and the tallest look good in the back. The dwarf and medium-height varieties can be used in planters. Trailing varieties do well in hanging baskets.

Recommended

There are many cultivars of *A. majus* available, generally grouped into three size categories: dwarf, medium and giant.

Snapdragons may survive the winter, but they grow best when they're planted annually.

Features: entertaining, colorful summer flowers
Flower color: white, cream, yellow, orange, red, maroon, pink, purple or bicolored **Height:** 6"–4' (15 cm–1.2 m)
Spread: 6–24" (15–60 cm)

Sunflower

Helianthus

'Teddy Bear' (above), common sunflower (below)

Birds will flock to the ripening seedheads of your sunflowers and quickly pluck out the tightly packed seeds.

The image of sunflowers against a weathered barn or tall garden shed has inspired artists of all ages throughout history.

Growing

Sunflowers grow best in **full sun**. The soil should be of **average fertility, humus rich, moist** and **well drained**.

The annual sunflower is an excellent plant for children to grow. The seeds are big and easy to handle, and they germinate quickly. The plant's upward growth can be measured until the flower blooms on top.

Tips

The lower-growing varieties can be used in beds and borders. The tall varieties are effective at the back of borders and make good screens and temporary hedges. The tallest varieties may need staking.

Carefree gardeners let sunflowers go to seed in the garden to produce new blooms the following summer.

Recommended

H. annuus (common sunflower) is considered weedy, but it has produced many attractive new cultivars.

Features: late-summer flowers, edible seeds **Flower color:** most commonly yellow, but also orange, red, brown, cream or bicolored; typically with brown, purple or rusty red centers **Height:** dwarf varieties, 24" (60 cm); giants up to 15' (4.5 m) **Spread:** 12–24" (30–60 cm)

Sweet Alyssum
Lobularia

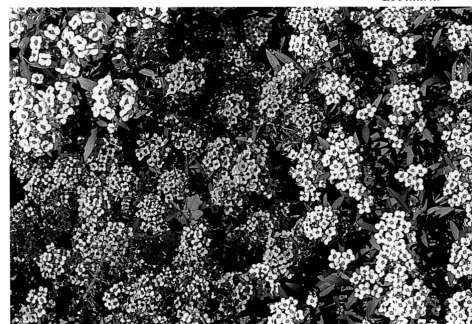

Sweet alyssum makes a lovely carpet of blooms to weave through formal and informal plantings. It is excellent for creating soft edges in beds and borders and along pathways.

Growing
Sweet alyssum prefers **full sun** but tolerates light shade. **Well-drained** soil of **average fertility** is preferred, but poor soil is tolerated. Sweet alyssum may die back a bit during hot and humid summers. Trim it back and water it periodically to encourage new growth and more flowers when the weather cools.

Tips
Sweet alyssum creeps around rock gardens, over rock walls and along the edges of beds. It is an excellent choice for seeding into cracks and crevices of walkways and between patio stones. Once established it readily reseeds. It is also good for filling spaces between taller plants in borders and mixed containers.

Recommended
L. maritima forms a low, spreading mound of foliage. The entire plant appears to be covered in tiny blossoms when in full flower. Cultivars are available in a wide range of flower colors.

Features: fragrant flowers **Flower color:** pink, purple, yellow, salmon, white **Height:** 3–12" (8–30 cm) **Spread:** 6–24" (15–60 cm)

Sweet Potato Vine
Ipomoea

'Margarita' (above & below)

This vigorous rambling plant has lime green, bruised purple or green, pink and cream variegated leaves, and can make any gardener look like a genius.

Growing
Grow sweet potato vine in **full sun**. Any type of soil will do, but a **light, well-drained** soil of **poor fertility** is preferred.

Tips
Sweet potato vine is a great addition to mixed planters, window boxes and hanging baskets. It will scramble around a rock garden and cascade over the edge of a retaining wall. These cascading plants can also be trained to grow up a trellis.

Recommended
I. batatas (sweet potato vine) is best recognized by its large, lime green, heart-shaped leaves. Cultivars are available in shades of purple and with different leaf shapes. A variety with tri-colored foliage is also available. Unlike the more aggressive members of the family, this species has a very civilized look. It drapes neatly over the sides of containers and spreads over the soil beneath taller plants.

Features: decorative foliage **Flower color:** grown for foliage **Height:** about 12" (30 cm) **Spread:** up to 15' (5 m) for the species; cultivars spread 4–6' (1.2–1.8 m)

Verbena
Verbena

V. canadensis (above), *V.* x *hybrida* (below)

This annual demands dry, well-drained soil, so it is best grown on sunny mounds, along raised median strips and with plants that suck moisture out of the soil, such as junipers.

Growing

Verbenas grow best in **full sun**. The soil should be **fertile** and **very well drained**. Pinch back young plants for bushy growth.

Tips

Use verbenas on rock walls and in beds, borders, rock gardens, containers, hanging baskets and window boxes. They make good substitutes for ivy-leaved geranium where the sun is hot and where a roof overhang keeps the mildew-prone verbenas dry.

Recommended

V. bonariensis forms a low clump of foliage from which tall, stiff stems bear clusters of small, purple flowers.

V. canadensis 'Homestead Purple' is a very vigorous plant that may come back the following spring in mild winter areas.

V. x *hybrida* is a bushy plant that may be upright or spreading. It bears clusters of small flowers in a wide range of colors. Cultivars are available.

Cut plants back by one-half in mid-summer to encourage lots of fall blooms.

Also called: garden verbena **Features:** summer flowers **Flower color:** red, pink, purple, blue, yellow, scarlet, silver, peach or white; some with white centers **Height:** 8"–5' (20 cm–1.5 m) **Spread:** 1–3' (30–90 cm)

Viola

Viola

Pansies (above), Johnny-jump-up (below)

Viola is a cottage garden staple. Two of its most popular species—pansies and Johnny-jump-ups—reseed and create a dazzling display in odd places such as gravel driveways, between evergreen shrubs and in sidewalk cracks.

Growing

Violas prefer **full sun** but tolerate partial shade. The soil should be **fertile, moist** and **well drained**.

Sow seeds indoors in early winter for spring flowers and in mid-summer for fall and early-winter blooms. More seeds will germinate if they are kept in darkness until they sprout.

Violas do best when the weather is cool and they may die back completely in hot summers. Plants may rejuvenate in fall, but it is often easier to plant new ones and ensure your garden looks its best.

Tips

Violas can be used in beds, borders and containers, and look great mixed in with spring-flowering bulbs.

Recommended

V. tricolor (Johnny-jump-up) is a popular species. The flowers are purple, white and yellow, usually in combination, although several varieties have flowers in a single color, often purple.

V. x *wittrockiana* (pansy) comes in blue, purple, red, orange, yellow, pink and white, often multi-colored or with face-like markings. Many cultivars are available.

Features: colorful flowers, easy to grow
Flower color: blue, purple, red, orange, yellow, pink, white, multi-colored **Height:** 3–10"
(8–25 cm) **Spread:** 6–12" (15–30 cm)

Anemone
Anemone

Japanese anemone (above & below)

Often considered some of the most beautiful and earliest spring flowers, anemones are also some of the last plants to continue flowering in late fall.

Growing

Anemones grow well in **sun or partial shade** in **humus-rich, moist, well-drained** soil. Divide in early spring or late fall, and grow them in containers for a year before planting them back in the garden in spring.

Tips

Anemones make beautiful additions to lightly shaded borders, woodland gardens and rock gardens. They look magnificent when planted en masse. Plant Japanese anemone behind shrubby roses to support the tall stems.

Recommended

A. blanda (Grecian windflower) produces blue flowers in spring. Its cultivars are available in white, pink and blue. Grow them in full sun and keep them dry during summer dormancy.

A. x *hybrida* (Japanese anemone) is an upright, suckering hybrid that bears pink or white flowers. Many cultivars are available.

A. sylvestris (snowdrop anemone) does well in woodland settings. Late-spring flowers are white with yellow centers.

Japanese anemones are beautiful plants that bloom at the end of summer when other flowers are fading.

Also called: windflower **Features:** attractive flowers and foliage **Flower color:** pink, red, purple, blue, yellow, white **Height:** 6"–5' (15 cm–1.5 m) **Spread:** 6–24" (15–60 cm) **Hardiness:** zones 5–8

Artemisia

Artemisia

Most of the artemisias are valued for their foliage, not their flowers. Silver is the ultimate blending color in the garden because it enhances every hue combined with it.

Growing

Artemisias grow best in **full sun**, in **well-drained** soil of **low to average fertility**. Rich soil causes lanky, invasive growth. Atemisias are very drought tolerant.

Artemisias respond well to pruning in late spring. If you prune before May, frost may kill any new growth. When they look straggly, cut them back hard to encourage new growth and maintain a neater form. Divide these plants every year or two.

Tips

Use artemisias in rock gardens and borders. Their foliage makes a good backdrop for brightly colored flowers. Smaller forms may be used to create knot gardens.

Recommended

A variety of artemisias are available; check your local garden center. Favorites include the following: ***A. ludoviciana* cultivars** (white sage, silver sage) are vigorous, upright, clump-forming plants, hardy to zone 4. ***A. schmidtiana*** (silvermound artemisia) is a low, dense, mound-forming plant with feathery foliage. **'Nana'** (dwarf silvermound) is very compact. ***A. stelleriana*** (beach wormwood) is a small plant that tolerates oceanside salt spray.

White sage (above & below)

Also called: wormwood, sage **Features:** silvery gray, feathery or deeply lobed foliage **Flower color:** plant grown for foliage **Height:** 6"–6' (15 cm–1.8 m) **Spread:** 12–36" (30–90 cm) **Hardiness:** zones 3–8

Aster
Aster

Purple and pink asters make a nice contrast to the yellow-flowered perennials common in the late-summer garden. You will also have birds, butterflies and bees arriving for a late-summer or fall garden party.

Growing
Asters prefer **full sun** but tolerate partial shade. The soil should be **fertile, moist** and **well drained**. In colder areas, mulch plants in winter to protect from temperature fluctuations. Divide every two to three years to maintain vigor and control spread. Plants will decline rapidly if not divided frequently.

Tips
Plant asters in the middle of borders and in cottage gardens, or naturalize them in wild gardens.

Recommended
Many species and cultivars are available. The following are the two most popular species. Check with your local garden center to see what is available.

A. novae-angliae (Michaelmas daisy, New England aster) is an upright, spreading, clump-forming perennial that bears yellow-centered, purple flowers.

A. novi-belgii (Michaelmas daisy, New York aster) is a dense, upright, clump-forming perennial with purple flowers.

New York aster (above & below)

In early spring and again in late spring, use hedge shears to cut back bushy, compact aster plants. These generally don't need staking and have reduced disease problems.

Features: late-summer to mid-autumn flowers
Flower color: red, white, blue, purple, pink; often with yellow centers **Height:** 10 "–5' (25 cm–1.5 m) **Spread:** 18–36" (45–90 cm)
Hardiness: zones 3–8

Astilbe

Astilbe

Arend's astilbe (above & below)

Astilbes are beacons in the shade. Their high-impact flowers will brighten any gloomy section of your garden.

Growing

Astilbes grow best in **light shade** or **partial shade** in **fertile, humus-rich, acidic, moist, well-drained** soil. Heavy shade reduces flowering. Astilbes like moist soil in summer, but should not sit in standing water during winter while they are dormant.

Astilbe should be divided every three years or so to maintain plant vigor. Root masses may lift out of the soil as they mature. Add a layer of topsoil and mulch if this occurs, or lift the entire plant and replant it deeper.

Tips

Astilbes can be grown near the edges of bog gardens and ponds, in woodland gardens and shaded borders.

Recommended

A. x *arendsii* (astilbe, false spirea, Arend's astilbe) is a group of hybrids with many available cultivars.

A. chinensis (Chinese astilbe) is a dense, vigorous perennial that tolerates dry soil better than other astilbe species. Many cultivars are available.

A. japonica (Japanese astilbe) is a compact, clump-forming species, rarely grown in favor of its many cultivars.

Features: attractive foliage, summer flowers, interesting seedheads **Flower color:** white, pink, purple, peach, red **Height:** 10"–4' (25 cm–1.2 m) **Spread:** 8–36" (20–90 cm) **Hardiness:** zones 3–8

Bellflower

Campanula

Thanks to their wide range of heights and habits, it is possible to put bellflowers almost anywhere in the garden.

Growing

Bellflowers grow well in **full sun, partial shade** or **light shade**. The soil should be of **average to high fertility** and **well drained**. Mulch to keep roots cool and moist in summer and protected in winter, particularly if snow cover is inconsistent. Deadhead to prolong blooming.

Tips

Plant upright and mounding bellflowers in borders and cottage gardens. Use low, spreading and trailing bellflowers in rock gardens and on rock walls. Edge beds with the low-growing varieties.

Recommended

Many species, cultivars and hybrids of bellflower are available, with growth habits ranging from low and spreading to upright or trailing. The most common bellflower is *C. carpatica* (Carpathian bellflower), a spreading, mounding perennial bearing blue, white or purple flowers. Several cultivars are available.

C. lactiflora (milky bellflower), *C. persicifolia* (peach-leaved bellflower), *C. portenschlagiana* (Dalmatian bellflower) and *C. poscharskyana* (Serbian bellflower) are also popular choices.

Peach-leaved bellflower (above), Carpathian bellflower (below)

Divide bellflowers every few years in early spring or late summer, to keep plants vigorous and to prevent them from becoming invasive.

Features: spring, summer or autumn flowers; varied growing habits
Flower color: blue, white, purple, pink
Height: 4–72" (10 cm–1.8 m) **Spread:** 12–36" (30–90 cm) **Hardiness:** zones 3–7

Black-Eyed Susan

Rudbeckia

R. fulgida with purple coneflower (above), *R. nitida* 'Herbstonne' (below)

Black-eyed Susan is a tough, low-maintenance, long-lived perennial. Plant it wherever you want a casual look. Black-eyed Susan looks great in drifts.

Growing

Black-eyed Susans grow well in **full sun** or **partial shade**. The soil should be of **average fertility** and **well drained**. Some *Rudbeckia* species are touted as 'claybusters' for their tolerance of fairly heavy clay soils. Established plants are drought tolerant, but water them regularly all the same. Divide them in spring or fall, every three to five years.

Tips

Include these native plants in wildflower and natural gardens, beds and borders. Pinching the plants in June will result in shorter, bushier stands.

Recommended

R. fulgida is an upright, spreading plant bearing orange-yellow flowers with brown centers. **Var. *sullivantii* 'Goldsturm'** bears large, bright, golden yellow flowers.

R. laciniata (cutleaf coneflower) forms a large, open clump. The yellow flowers have green centers. **'Goldquelle'** has bright yellow, double flowers.

R. nitida is an upright, spreading plant with green-centered yellow flowers. **'Herbstonne'** (Autumn Sun) has bright, golden yellow flowers.

Features: bright flowers, attractive foliage, easy to grow **Flower color:** yellow, orange or red; centers are typically brown or green
Height: 24"–6' (60 cm–1.8 m) **Spread:** 18–36" (45–90 cm) **Hardiness:** zones 3–8

Bleeding Heart
Dicentra

*F*ew plants look as graceful in the garden as bleeding hearts. Every garden should have a spot for one.

Growing

Bleeding hearts prefer **partial to light shade** but will grow in full sun or full shade. The soil should be **humus rich, moist** and **well drained**. Very dry summer conditions cause the plants to die back, though they will revive in fall or the following spring. Regular watering will keep the flowers blooming until mid-summer. *D. eximia* and *D. spectabilis* rarely need dividing. *D. formosa* can be divided every three years or so.

Tips

Bleeding hearts can be naturalized in a woodland garden or grown in a border or rock garden. They make excellent early-season specimen plants and do well near ponds or streams.

All bleeding hearts contain toxic alkaloids, and some people develop allergic skin reactions from contact with these plants.

Recommended

Three common species are **D. eximia** (fringed bleeding heart), **D. formosa** (western bleeding heart) and **D. spectabilis** (common bleeding heart, Japanese bleeding heart). Several cultivars of *D. spectabilis* are available. *D. eximia* is the most drought tolerant and most likely to continue flowering all summer.

Western bleeding heart (above), common bleeding heart (below)

Bleeding hearts are mound-forming plants with delicate, fern-like foliage.

Features: spring and summer flowers, attractive foliage **Flower color:** pink, white, red, purple **Height:** 12"–4' (30 cm–1.2 m) **Spread:** 12–36" (30–90 cm) **Hardiness:** zones 3–9

Catmint

Nepeta

H. x faassenii (above & below)

The real workhorses of the garden bed, catmints offer season-long blooms on sturdy, trouble-free plants.

Growing

These plants prefer **full sun** in coastal areas and **partial shade** inland. Grow them in **well-drained** soil of **average fertility**; the growth tends to flop in rich soil. Plant in spring and divide in spring or fall when they look overgrown and dense.

In June, pinch the tips to delay flowering and make the plants more compact.

Tips

Catmints form upright, spreading clumps. Plant them in herb gardens, perennial beds, rock gardens and cottage gardens with roses. Or use them to edge borders and pathways.

Take care if you decide to grow *N. cataria* (catnip) because cats are extremely attracted to this plant. Cats do like the other species, but not as much.

Recommended

N. **'Blue Beauty'** (Souvenir d'André Chaudron) has gray-green foliage and large, dark, purple-blue flowers.

N. x ***faassenii*** bears blue or purple flowers. Cultivars with gray-green foliage and pink, white, light purple or lavender blue flowers are available, as well as low-growing cultivars.

N. **'Six Hills Giant'** bears deep lavender blue flowers.

Features: aromatic foliage, attractive flowers, easy to grow **Flower color:** blue, purple, white, pink **Height:** 18–36" (45–90 cm) **Spread:** 12–24" (30–60 cm) **Hardiness:** zones 3–8

Columbine

Aquilegia

Delicate but long-lasting columbine flowers herald the passing of spring and the arrival of warm summer weather.

Growing

Columbines grow well in **full sun** or **partial shade**. They prefer **fertile, moist** and **well-drained** soil, but they adapt to most soil conditions. Division is not required but can be done to propagate desirable plants. The divided plants may take a while to recover because columbines dislike having their roots disturbed.

Tips

Use columbines in rock gardens, formal or casual borders and naturalized or woodland gardens.

Recommended

A. alpina has blue flowers.

A. canadensis (wild columbine, Canada columbine) and *A. formosa* are native Canadian plants common in woodlands and fields. They bear yellow flowers with red spurs.

A. x hybrida (*A.* x *cultorum*; hybrid columbine) has exceptional flowers. Hybrids in a wide range of colors have been developed.

A. vulgaris (European columbine, common columbine) has been used to develop many hybrids and cultivars with flowers in various colors.

Common columbine 'Nora Barlow' (above), hybrid columbine (below)

Columbines self-seed but are not invasive. Each year, a few new seedlings may turn up near the parent plant and can be transplanted.

Features: spring and summer flowers, attractive foliage **Flower color:** red, yellow, pink, purple, blue, white; color of spurs often differs from that of the petals **Height:** 18–36" (45–90 cm) **Spread:** 12–24" (30–60 cm) **Hardiness:** zones 3–8

Coral Bells

Heuchera

These delicate woodland plants will enhance your garden with their bright colors, attractive foliage and airy sprays of flowers.

Growing

Grow coral bells in **full sun** or **partial shade** because they won't flower if shade is too heavy. Soil should be **average to fertile, neutral or slightly alkaline, evenly moist** and **well drained**.

Deadhead to prolong the blooming period. Every two or three years in spring or fall, dig up plants to remove the oldest, woodiest roots and stems. Divide the plants at this time if desired, then replant the crowns just above soil level.

Coral bells may push themselves up out of the soil. Mulch plants in fall if they begin heaving from the ground.

Tips

Use coral bells as edging plants, in clusters in woodland gardens or as groundcovers in low-traffic areas. Combine different foliage types for an interesting display.

Recommended

Many coral bells species, cultivars and hybrids exist, providing a range of sizes, flower colors and foliage colors and shapes. Check with your local garden center or nursery.

Features: colorful foliage, easy to grow **Flower color:** red, pink, white
Height: 12" (30 cm) **Spread:** 12" (30 cm) **Hardiness:** zones 3–8

Daylily
Hemerocallis

The daylily's adaptability and durability combined with its variety in color, blooming period, size and texture explain this perennial's popularity.

Growing

Daylilies grow in any light from **full sun to partial shade**. The deeper the shade, the fewer flowers will be produced. The soil should be **fertile, moist** and **well drained**. These plants adapt to most conditions and are hard to kill once established. Divide every two to three years to keep plants vigorous and to propagate them. They can be left indefinitely without dividing.

Tips

Plant daylilies alone, or group them in borders, on banks and in ditches to control erosion. They can be naturalized in woodland or meadow gardens. Small varieties look nice in planters.

Deadhead to prolong blooming. Be careful when deadheading purple-flowered daylilies because the sap can stain fingers and clothes.

Recommended

Daylilies come in an almost infinite number of forms, sizes and colors, in a range of species, cultivars and hybrids. See your local garden center or daylily grower to find out what's available and what suits your garden.

Easygoing, adaptive and versatile, daylilies are so tough they can even be dug up and moved while in full bloom.

Features: spring and summer flowers, grass-like foliage, easy to grow
Flower color: every color except blue and pure white **Height:** 12"–4' (30 cm–1.2 m)
Spread: 12"–4' (30 cm–1.2 m)
Hardiness: zones 2–8

Euphorbia

Euphorbia

'Fireglow' (above), *E. polychroma* (below)

These mounding plants are admired for the brightly colored bracts that surround their tiny flowers. A second show of color appears in fall when the leaves turn purple, red or orange.

Growing

Euphorbia grows well in **full sun** or **light shade,** in **moist, well-drained, humus-rich** soil of **average fertility**. These plants are drought tolerant and can be invasive in fertile soil. They do not tolerate wet conditions. Plant them in spring or fall.

Propagate euphorbia with stem cuttings. Dip the cut ends in hot water to stop the sticky white sap from running.

Division is rarely required. These plants dislike being disturbed once established.

Tips

Use euphorbia in a mixed or herbaceous border, rock garden or lightly shaded woodland garden.

Recommended

E. griffithii 'Fireglow' has light green leaves, orange stems and bright orange bracts.

E. polychroma (*E. epithimoides*) has inconspicuous flowers surrounded by long-lasting, yellow bracts. It has several cultivars.

Also called: cushion spurge **Features:** colorful bracts, fall foliage, low maintenance
Flower color: yellow **Height:** 30–60 cm (12–24") **Spread:** 45–60 cm (18–24")
Hardiness: zones 4–8

Foamflower
Tiarella

Foamflowers form handsome ground-covers in shaded areas, with attractive leaves and delicate, starry, white flowers.

Growing

Foamflowers prefer **partial, light or full shade** without afternoon sun. The soil should be **humus rich, moist** and **slightly acidic.** These plants adapt to most soils.

Divide in spring. Deadhead to encourage reblooming. If the foliage fades or rusts in summer, cut it partway to the ground. New growth will emerge.

Tips

Foamflowers are excellent groundcovers for shaded and woodland gardens. They can be included in shaded borders and left to naturalize in wild gardens.

Recommended

T. cordifolia is a low-growing, spreading plant that bears spikes of foamy-looking, white flowers.

T. laciniata is a Pacific Northwest native that bears white flowers in summer.

T. 'Maple Leaf' is a clump-forming hybrid with bronze-green, maple-like leaves and pink-flushed flowers.

T. trifoliata is another Pacific Northwest native with pendent white flowers borne in late spring to mid-summer. '**Incardine**' has pink flowers.

New varieties of foamflowers are flooding the market with spectacular leaf color. Some have bands, splotches and rings.

T. cordifolia (above & below)

Don't worry about foamflower taking over the garden. It spreads rather politely by underground stolons, and is easily pulled up if it wanders too enthusiastically.

Features: spring and sometimes early-summer flowers, decorative foliage **Flower color:** white, pink **Height:** 4–24" (10–60 cm) **Spread:** 12–24" (30–60 cm) **Hardiness:** zones 3–8

Goat's Beard

Aruncus

Despite its imposing size, goat's beard has a soft and delicate appearance, with divided foliage and large, plumy, cream flowers.

Growing

These plants prefer **partial to full shade**; in deep shade, they bear fewer blooms. They tolerate full sun as long as the soil is kept evenly moist. Provide protection from hot afternoon sun. Soil should be **fertile, moist** and **humus rich**.

Divide in spring or autumn. Use a sharp knife or an axe to cut the dense root mass into pieces. Fortunately, these plants rarely need dividing.

Tips

These plants look very natural growing on the edge of a woodland garden, in a native plant garden or in a large island planting. They may also be used in a border or alongside a stream or pond.

Recommended

A. aethusifolius (dwarf Korean goat's beard) forms a low-growing, compact mound and bears branched spikes of loosely held, cream flowers.

A. dioicus (giant goat's beard, common goat's beard) is a large, bushy, shrub-like perennial with large plumes of creamy white flowers. There are several cultivars.

Giant goat's beard (above & below)

Features: early- to mid-summer blooms, shrub-like habit, attractive foliage and seed-heads **Flower color:** cream, white
Height: 6"–6' (15 cm–1.8 m)
Spread: 12"–6' (30 cm–1.8 m)
Hardiness: zones 3–8

Golden Marguerite

Anthemis

Grow golden marguerite to give your garden a casual cottage appearance.

Growing

Golden marguerite prefers **full sun** and **average to poor, well-drained** soil. This plant is drought tolerant. The clumps tend to die out in the middle and should be divided every two or three years in spring or fall. Plant them in spring.

These plants flower in waves. Dead-heading will encourage flowering all summer and greatly reduce self-seeding. Cut back thin-looking plants to promote new growth and flowers. To avoid staking, cut plants back in May or group several plants to support each other. To support the stems as they grow, insert twiggy branches into the soil around the plants when they are young.

Tips

Marguerites form attractive clumps that blend wonderfully into cottage-style gardens. Their drought tolerance makes them ideal for use in rock gardens and on exposed slopes.

Recommended

A. tinctoria forms a mounded clump of foliage that becomes completely covered in daisy-like flowers in summer. Its cultivars bloom in shades of orange and yellow.

Also called: Marguerite daisy
Features: colorful flowers **Flower color:** yellow, orange, cream **Height:** 24–36" (60–90 cm) **Spread:** 24–36" (60–90 cm) **Hardiness:** zones 3–7

Golden marguerites look great as cut flowers placed in anything from vases to tin cans and old teapots.

Hardy Geranium

Geranium

Bloodred cranesbill (above & below)

Thanks to the beauty and diversity of this hardy plant, there is a type of geranium that suits every garden.

Growing

Hardy geraniums grow well in **full sun, partial shade** and **light shade**. These plants dislike hot weather and prefer soil of **average fertility** and **good drainage**. *G. renardii* prefers a poor, well-drained soil. Divide in spring.

Tips

These long-flowering plants work well in a border; they fill in the spaces between shrubs and other larger plants, and keep weeds down. Include them in rock gardens and woodland gardens, or mass plant them as groundcovers.

Recommended

G. **'Brookside'** is a clump-forming, drought-tolerant geranium with finely cut leaves and deep blue to violet blue flowers.

G. macrorrhizum (bigroot geranium, scented cranesbill) forms a spreading mound of fragrant foliage with flowers in various shades of pink.

G. renardii (Renard's geranium) forms a clump of velvety, deeply veined, crinkled foliage. A few purple-veined white flowers appear over the summer.

G. sanguineum (bloodred cranesbill, bloody cranesbill) forms a dense, mounding clump and bears bright magenta flowers.

Also called: cranesbill geranium **Features:** summer flowers; attractive, sometimes fragrant foliage **Flower color:** white, red, pink, purple, blue **Height:** 4–36" (10–90 cm) **Spread:** 12–36" (30–90 cm) **Hardiness:** zones 3–8

Hosta

Hosta

Breeders are always looking for new variations in hosta foliage. Swirls, stripes, puckers and ribs enhance the leaves' various sizes, shapes and colors.

Growing

Hostas prefer **light shade to partial shade** but will grow in full shade. Morning sun is preferable to afternoon sun. The soil should ideally be **fertile, moist** and **well drained**, but most soils are tolerated. Hostas are fairly drought tolerant, especially if mulched to help retain moisture.

Division is not required but can be done every few years in spring or summer to propagate new plants.

Tips

Hostas make wonderful woodland plants and look very attractive when combined with ferns and other fine-textured plants. Hostas work well in mixed borders, particularly when used to hide leggy lower stems and branches of some shrubs. Hostas' dense growth and thick, shade-providing leaves help suppress weeds.

Recommended

There are hundreds of hosta species, cultivars and hybrids. Visit your local garden center or get a mail-order catalogue to find out what's available.

Some gardeners think the flowers clash with the foliage, and they remove the newly emerged flower stems. Doing so won't harm the plant.

Also called: plantain lily
Features: decorative foliage, summer and autumn flowers **Flower color:** white or purple; plants grown mainly for foliage
Height: 4–36" (10–90 cm) **Spread:** 6"–6' (15 cm–1.8 m) **Hardiness:** zones 3–8

Iris

Iris

Siberian iris (above), bearded iris (below)

Cut bearded iris foliage to within a few inches of the ground in mid-summer to discourage leaf spot and other fungal diseases.

Irises are old-fashioned flowers that bring back childhood memories of Grandma's spring garden.

Growing

Irises prefer **full sun** but tolerate very light or dappled shade. The soil should be of **average fertility** and **well drained**. Japanese iris and Siberian iris prefer moist, well-drained soil.

Divide irises in late summer or early autumn. Deadhead to keep them tidy. Cut back Siberian iris' foliage in spring.

Tips

All irises are popular border plants. Japanese and Siberian iris grow well alongside streams or ponds. Dwarf cultivars look attractive in rock gardens.

Irises can cause severe internal irritation if ingested. Always wash your hands after handling them. Avoid planting irises where children play.

Recommended

Many species and hybrids are available. Among the most popular is **bearded iris**, often a hybrid of *I. germanica*. It has the widest range of flower colors, but is susceptible to iris borer. Several irises are not susceptible, including *I. ensata* (Japanese iris) and *I. siberica* (Siberian iris). **Pacific Coast hybrids** come in many colors and sizes.

Features: spring, summer and sometimes autumn flowers; attractive foliage **Flower color:** many shades of pink, red, purple, blue, white, brown, yellow **Height:** 4"–4' (10 cm–1.2 m) **Spread:** 2"–4' (5 cm–1.2 m) **Hardiness:** zones 3–8

Lady's Mantle
Alchemilla

This plant is treasured as much for its foliage as for its flowers. Delicate sprays of flowers veil the slightly cupped leaves, which collect dewdrops that glisten like diamonds.

Growing

Lady's mantle grows well in **full sun** or **light shade**. Protect it from direct sun in hot locations. It prefers to grow in a **rich, moist** soil amended with lots of **organic matter**. It is drought resistant once established. Plant it in spring.

If lady's mantle begins to look tired and heat-stressed during summer, cut it back lightly to rejuvenate it. Deadhead to reduce self-seeding and encourage a second flush of flowers.

Tips

Lady's mantle works well grouped under trees in a woodland garden or along a border edge where it can soften the other plants' bright colors.

Recommended

A. alpina is a popular small version of lady's mantle.

A. mollis (common lady's mantle) forms a mound of soft, rounded foliage.

Common lady's mantle (above & below)

Established plants will not likely need dividing, but it can be done in early spring before flowering, if desired. Self-seeded seedlings may be moved to other locations.

Features: foliage, delicate flowers
Flower color: chartreuse **Height:** 4–18" (10–45 cm) **Spread:** 12–24" (30–60 cm) **Hardiness:** zones 3–7

Lamium

Lamium

'Limelight' (above), 'Beacon Silver' (below)

With their striking, variegated leaves, lamium brighten up dark spaces in the garden. They look especially lovely at dusk and in the moonlight.

Growing
Lamium prefer **partial to light shade**. They tolerate full shade but may grow leggy. The soil should be of **average fertility, humus rich, moist** and **well drained**. The more fertile the soil, the more vigorously the plants will grow.

Lamium are drought tolerant when grown in shade, but can develop bare patches if the soil is allowed to dry out for extended periods. Divide and replant them in fall if bare spots become unsightly. Plant in spring or fall.

Tips
These plants make useful groundcovers in woodland or shade gardens. Or try planting them under shrubs in a border, where they will help keep weeds down.

Recommended
L. maculatum (spotted dead nettle) is a low-growing, spreading plant with white, pink or mauve flowers. Many cultivars are available.

Also called: dead nettle, spotted dead nettle
Features: foliage, flowers **Flower color:** white, pink, red-purple **Height:** 8" (20 cm)
Spread: 36" (90 cm) **Hardiness:** zones 3–8

Lungwort

Pulmonaria

A wide variety of lungworts are available, with highly attractive foliage ranging in color from apple green to silver-spotted olive to dark emerald.

Growing

Lungworts prefer **partial to full shade**. The soil should be **fertile, humus rich, moist** and **well drained**. Rot can occur in very wet soil.

Divide after flowering in early summer or in fall. Ensure that newly planted divisions are kept moist to help them re-establish.

Tips

Lungworts make attractive groundcovers for shady borders, woodland gardens and pond and stream edges.

Recommended

P. longifolia (long-leaved lungwort) forms a dense clump of long, narrow, white-spotted green leaves and bears clusters of blue flowers.

P. officinalis (common lungwort, spotted dog) forms a loose clump of evergreen foliage spotted with white. The flowers open pink and then mature to blue. Cultivars are available.

P. saccharata (Bethlehem sage) forms a compact clump of large, white-spotted, evergreen leaves and purple, red or white flowers. Many cultivars are available.

There are other species, cultivars and hybrids available. Check with your local garden center.

Bethleham sage (above & below)

To keep lungworts tidy and show off the fabulous foliage, deadhead the plants by shearing them back lightly after flowering.

Features: decorative, mottled foliage; spring flowers
Flower color: blue, red, pink, white; plants also grown for foliage **Height:** 8–24" (20–60 cm)
Spread: 8–36" (20–90 cm) **Hardiness:** zones 3–8

Penstemon

Penstemon

'Husker Red' (above), 'Apple Blossom' (below)

Penstemon's colorful stalks will welcome hummingbirds and butterflies on a summer day.

Growing

Penstemons prefer **full sun** but tolerate some shade. The soil should be of **average to rich fertility, sandy** and **well drained.** Penstemons are drought tolerant and will rot in wet soil. Plant in spring or fall; divide every two or three years in spring.

To support the tall stems, insert twiggy branches in the soil around the plants in spring before they grow too tall. Pinch plants when they reach 12" (30 cm) tall to encourage bushy growth.

Tips

The attractive flowers make a lovely addition to a mixed border, cottage garden or rock garden.

Recommended

Penstemon has many species, cultivars and hybrids, which provide a range of flower colors, shapes and sizes. Check at your local garden center or nursery for availability. *P. digitalis* **'Husker Red'** is a recent Perennial Plant Association Perennial Plant of the Year. The bronze-red foliage contrasts well with its white flowers.

Also called: beard tongue **Features:** interesting flowers **Flower color:** white, yellow, light pink, rose pink, purple **Height:** 8–24" (20–60 cm) **Spread:** 10–12" (25–30 cm) **Hardiness:** zones 4–8

Peony
Paeonia

From the simple, single flowers to the extravagant doubles, it's easy to become mesmerized with these voluptuous plants. The foliage remains stellar throughout the growing season.

Growing

Peonies prefer **full sun** but tolerate some shade. Peonies like **fertile, humus-rich, moist, well-drained** soil with lots of compost. Prepare the soil before introducing the plants. Mulch peonies lightly with compost in spring. Too much fertilizer, particularly nitrogen, causes floppy growth and retards blooming. Peonies don't appreciate being divided. Deadhead to keep plants looking tidy.

Tips

Peonies look great in a border combined with other early bloomers. Avoid planting peonies under trees, where they have to compete for moisture and nutrients.

Peony tubers planted too shallow or too deep will not flower. The buds or eyes on the tuber should be $1^1/_3$–2" (3–5 cm) below the soil surface.

Place wire tomato or peony cages around the plants in early spring to support the heavy flowers. The growing foliage will hide the cage.

Recommended

Hundreds of peony varieties exist. Cultivars come in a wide range of colors, may have single or double flowers and may or may not be fragrant. Visit your local garden center to see what is available.

Garden peony (above & below)

Features: spring and early-summer flowers, attractive foliage **Flower color:** white, cream white, yellow, pink, red, purple **Height:** 24–36" (60–90 cm) **Spread:** 24–36" (60–90 cm) **Hardiness:** zones 2–8

Phlox
Phlox

P. paniculata (above & below)

The name Phlox comes from the Greek word for 'flame,' which reflects the vibrant flower colors of many species.

Phlox comes in many shapes and sizes, from low creepers to bushy border plants. Their flowering periods can fall anywhere between early spring and mid-autumn.

Growing
P. paniculata and *P. maculata* prefer **full sun**; *P. subulata* prefers **full sun to partial shade**; *P. stolonifera* prefers **light to partial shade** but tolerates heavy shade. All like **fertile, humus-rich, moist, well-drained** soil. Divide in autumn or spring.

Tips
Low-growing species are useful in rock gardens or at the front of borders. Taller phloxes may be used in the middle of borders and are particularly effective planted in groups.

Recommended
P. maculata (early phlox, garden phlox, wild sweet William) forms an upright clump of hairy stems and narrow leaves that are sometimes spotted with red. Pink, purple or white flowers are borne in conical clusters.

P. paniculata (garden phlox, summer phlox) is an upright plant. Its many cultivars vary in size and flower color.

P. stolonifera (creeping phlox) is a low, spreading plant that bears flowers in several shades of purple.

P. subulata (moss phlox, moss pink) is very low growing and bears flowers in various colors. The foliage is evergreen.

Features: spring, summer or autumn flowers **Flower color:** white, blue, purple, orange, pink, red **Height:** 2"–4' (5 cm–1.2 m) **Spread:** 12–36" (30–90 cm) **Hardiness:** zones 3–8

Pinks

Dianthus

Maiden pink (above), cottage pink (below)

From tiny and delicate to large and robust, this genus contains a wide variety of plants, many with spice-scented flowers.

Growing

Pinks prefer **full sun** but tolerate some light shade. A **well-drained, neutral or alkaline** soil is required. Ensure pinks have excellent drainage—they hate to stand in water.

Tips

Use pinks in rock gardens and rock walls, for edging borders and walkways, in cutting gardens and even as groundcovers. To prolong blooming, deadhead as the flowers fade, but leave a few flowers in place to go to seed.

Recommended

D. x *allwoodii* (allwood pink) forms a compact mound and bears flowers in a wide range of colors. Many cultivars are available.

D. deltoides (maiden pink) forms a mat of foliage and flowers in shades of red.

D. gratianopolitanus (cheddar pink) is long lived and forms a very dense mat of evergreen, silver gray foliage with sweet-scented flowers mostly in shades of pink.

D. plumarius (cottage pink) is noted for its role in the development of garden pinks. The flowers can be single, semi-double or fully double and come in many colors.

Features: sometimes-fragrant spring or summer flowers, attractive foliage **Flower color:** pink, red, white, purple **Height:** 2–18" (5–45 cm) **Spread:** 6–24" (15–60 cm) **Hardiness:** zones 3–9

Primrose

Primula

Pruhonicensis Hybrid (above), *P. capitata* (below)

Planted among dwarf daffodils, lungworts and pulmonarias, primroses add to a tapestry of woodland flowers. They are the jewels of the spring display.

Growing

Grow primrose in **partial shade, in moderately fertile, humus-rich, moist, well-drained, neutral to slightly acidic** soil. Overgrown clumps should be divided after flowering or in early fall. Plant in spring.

Pull off yellowing or dried leaves in fall to encourage fresh, new growth in spring.

Tips

Primroses work well in many areas of the garden. Some prefer woodland areas while others thrive in moisture. Species with flowers on tall stems look excellent in masses, while species with solitary flowers peeking out among the foliage add an interesting dimension to the garden.

If the temperature is too hot or too cold, primroses will stop blooming. Plant them in a variety of sites to increase your chances of success.

Recommended

The most popular primroses are **Polyantha Hybrids**, which are available in a wide range of solid colors or bicolors. Many species and cultivars are available, with colorful flowers and a variety of plant forms.

Features: colorful flowers, variety of forms
Flower color: red, orange, pink, purple, blue, white, yellow **Height:** 6–24" (15–60 cm) **Spread:** 6–18" (15–45 cm) **Hardiness:** zones 3–8

Purple Coneflower

Echinacea

Purple coneflower is a visual delight, with its mauve petals offset by a spiky, orange center.

Growing

Purple coneflower grows well in **full sun** or **very light shade**. It tolerates any **well-drained** soil, but prefers an **average to rich soil**. The thick taproots make this plant drought resistant, but it prefers to have regular water. Divide every four years or so in spring or autumn.

Deadhead early in the season to prolong flowering. Later, you may wish to leave the flowerheads in place to self-seed and provide winter interest. Pinch plants back or thin out the stems in early summer to encourage bushy growth that is less prone to mildew.

Tips

Use purple coneflowers in meadow gardens and informal borders, in groups or as single specimens.

The dry flowerheads make an interesting feature in autumn and winter gardens.

Recommended

E. purpurea is an upright plant covered in prickly hairs. It bears purple flowers with orangy centers. Cultivars are available.

E. purpurea with black-eyed Susan (above)

Purple coneflower attracts wildlife to the garden; it provides pollen, nectar and seeds for various hungry visitors.

Features: mid-summer to autumn flowers, persistent seedheads **Flower color:** purple, pink, white; rusty orange centers **Height:** 24–60" (60 cm–1.5 m) **Spread:** 12–24" (30–60 cm) **Hardiness:** zones 3–8

Rock Cress
Aubrieta

*R*ock cress is a wonderful plant that blooms in partially shaded rock outcroppings and can survive an onslaught of slugs.

Growing

Rock cress prefers **full sun** but tolerates partial shade. Soil should be of **average fertility, moist, neutral to slightly alkaline** and **well drained,** with rocks or gravel mixed in. Plant it in the fall.

Every year or two, in fall, divide the clump to prevent it from thinning and dying out in the middle. Shear rock cress back by one-half once it finishes flowering to encourage compact growth and the occasional second flush of flowers.

Tips

Use rock cress in rock wall crevices, between the paving stones of a pathway, in a rock garden, along the edge of a border or beneath taller plants.

Recommended

Many cultivars can be attributed to either *A.* x *cultorum* or *A. deltoidea.* All are low, mounding or cascading perennials that flower in early or mid-spring. Check with your local garden center for availability.

This low-grower can spread quite far but rarely becomes invasive in the garden.

Also called: common aubrieta **Features:** flowers, foliage, form **Flower color:** white, rose pink or purple **Height:** 2–6" (5–15 cm) **Spread:** 24" (60 cm) or wider **Hardiness:** zones 5–7

Sea Pink

Armeria

Sea pink is the perfect plant to grow in pots at an oceanside cabin, where it can add tufts of texture to a sunny rock garden or alongside a flagstone path. The rounded blossoms blend well with other drought-tolerant plants with gray foliage. This tough perennial can survive neglect.

Growing

Sea pink requires **full sun.** Soil should be **poor to moderate** and **well drained.** Sea pink is very drought tolerant. If it seems to be dying out in the middle of the clump, try cutting it back hard. New shoots should fill in quickly. Plant sea pink in spring and divide it in spring or fall.

Tips

Sea pink is great for seaside gardens because it tolerates salt spray. Use this little gem in a rock garden or at the front of a border.

Recommended

A. **'Bee's Ruby'** is a larger cultivar with bright pink flowers.

*A. **maritima*** is the most common and most variable sea pink. The flowering stems rise above the tufts of foliage.

A. maritima (above & below)

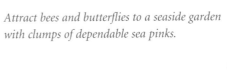

Attract bees and butterflies to a seaside garden with clumps of dependable sea pinks.

Also called: common thrift
Features: flowers, foliage, salt tolerance **Flower color:** shades of pink, red, white **Height:** 6–18" (15–45 cm) **Spread:** 8–12" (20–30 cm) **Hardiness:** zones 3–8

Wild Ginger
Asarum

Canadian wild ginger (above), European wild ginger (below)

Wild ginger flowers have a unique shape, an unusual brown-maroon color and an unpleasant, slightly fetid odor that attracts their beetle pollinators.

Wild ginger is a beautiful ground-cover for woodland sites. Glossy, heart-shaped leaves form a low-growing mat that grows quickly but is not invasive.

Growing

Wild gingers need **full or partial shade**. The soil should be **moist** and **humus rich**. All *Asarum* species prefer acidic soils, but *A. canadense* will tolerate alkaline conditions. Wild gingers tolerate dry conditions for a while in good shade, but prolonged drought will eventually cause wilt and dieback.

Tips

Use wild ginger in a shady rock garden, border or woodland garden. Wild ginger is relatively easy to remove from places in which it isn't welcome.

Recommended

A. canadense (Canada wild ginger) has slightly hairy, heart-shaped leaves. The roots of this wild ginger can be used in place of true ginger (*Zingiber officinale*) in recipes.

A. caudatum (British Columbia wild ginger) prefers cooler summer growing conditions.

A. europaeum (European wild ginger) forms an expanding clump of very glossy leaves, often distinctively silver-veined. This species is not as heat tolerant as *A. canadense*.

A. hartwegii bears dark green leaves with white, mottled veins.

Features: attractive foliage, easy to grow
Flower color: inconspicuous flowers are burgundy or green; plant grown for foliage **Height:** 3–6" (8–15 cm) **Spread:** 12" (30 cm) or more
Hardiness: zones 4–8

Arborvitae

Thuja

Arborvitae makes a gorgeous backdrop for perennial and shrub borders. Rot-resistant, durable and long-lived, arborvitae has earned the admiration of gardeners everywhere.

Growing

Arborvitae prefers **full sun.** The soil should be of **average fertility, moist** and **well drained.** These plants enjoy humidity and grow well near marshy areas. Provide some shelter from strong or frequent winds.

Tips

Larger varieties of arborvitae make excellent specimen trees. Smaller cultivars can be used in foundation plantings, in shrub and mixed borders, as formal or informal hedges and in rock gardens. Varieties with yellow foliage add color to the winter landscape.

Deer enjoy eating the foliage of eastern arborvitae. Western arborvitae is relatively resistant to deer browsing.

Recommended

T. occidentalis (American arborvitae, eastern arborvitae) is a dense, broad, pyramidal tree. (Zones 2–7; cultivars are not always this cold hardy.)

T. orientalis (*Platycladus orientalis*, Oriental arborvitae) is a pyramidal to columnar, large shrub or small tree. (Zones 5–8)

American arborvitae 'Yellow Ribbon' (above), American arborvitae (below)

T. plicata (western red cedar, western arborvitae) is a very large, often multi-stemmed, narrow, pyramidal tree. (Zones 5–7)

The pungent oils in this tree's foliage may irritate sensitive skin.

Also called: cedar **Features:** foliage, bark, form
Habit: small to large evergreen tree
Height: 3–75' (1–23 m) **Spread:** 3–25' (1–7.5 m)
Hardiness: zones 2–8

Arbutus
Arbutus

A. menziesii (above & below)

*A*rbutus trees grow wild along the Pacific coast, often on rocky cliffs overlooking the water. The peeling bark, interesting twisted and irregular forms, clusters of white flowers in early summer and bright red fruit that attracts plenty of birds provide more than enough reason to grow this Pacific beauty.

Growing
Arbutus prefers a **sheltered** spot in **full sun.** The soil should be **fertile, humus rich** and **well drained.** Avoid overwatering these trees, which are drought and salt tolerant. Pruning is not usually required.

Arbutus do not like having their roots disturbed. Plant young stock and make sure the location is a permanent one.

Tips
Use arbutus in a woodland garden or as specimen trees. Include the smaller cultivars in shrub or mixed borders.

Recommended
A. **'Marina'** has large, green leaves, rosy pink flowers and red and yellow fruit.

A. menziesii (arbutus, Pacific madrone) is a large, spreading or shrubby tree with distinctive reddish bark that continuously peels off to reveal smooth, greenish young bark underneath.

A. unedo (Mediterranean strawberry tree) is a spreading, shrubby tree with shredding, exfoliating red-brown bark.

Also called: strawberry tree, madrone
Features: flowers, fruit, bark, form **Habit:** spreading or shrubby, broad-leaved, evergreen tree **Height:** 5–70' (1.5–21 m) **Spread:** 5–70' (1.5–21 m) **Hardiness:** zones 7–8

Barberry
Berberis

Darwin's barberry (above & below)

arberries are dependable, easy-growing shrubs with many variations in plant size, foliage color and fruit.

Growing
Barberries develop the best fall color and most fruit when grown in **full sun**, but they tolerate partial shade. Any **well-drained** soil is suitable. Barberries tolerate drought and urban conditions but suffer in poorly drained, wet soil.

Tips
Large barberries make great hedges. They can also be included in shrub and mixed borders. Small cultivars can be grown in rock gardens, in raised beds and along rock walls.

Recommended
B. darwinii (Darwin's barberry) bears small yellow flowers in spring and often again in fall, and small, dark blue berries. This evergreen species is not as spiny as others.

B. x *mentorensis* (Mentor barberry) is a large, generally deciduous shrub with even, dense growth, impassable spines, yellow spring flowers and attractive fall color.

B. thunbergii (Japanese barberry) is a broad, rounded, dense shrub with bright green foliage, orange, red or purple fall color, yellow spring flowers and glossy red fruit. Many cultivars have varied foliage color, including shades of purple and yellow. Variegated varieties also exist.

Features: foliage, flowers, fruit, formidable spines **Habit:** prickly deciduous shrub
Height: 12"–6' (30 cm–1.8 m) **Spread:** 18"–6' (45–1.8 m) **Hardiness:** zones 4–8

Bluebeard
Caryopteris

Bluebeard is a cheerful, easy-to-grow shrub that will wake up a late-summer border with its blue flowers. The flowers and foliage contrast superbly with purple-leaved plants.

Growing
Bluebeard prefers **full sun** but tolerates light shade. It does best in soil of **average fertility** that is **light** and **well drained**.

Tips
Include bluebeard in your shrub or mixed border. This plant can be treated as a herbaceous perennial in areas where it is killed back each winter.

Recommended
C. x *clandonensis* forms a dense mound and bears clusters of blue or purple flowers in late summer and early fall. **'Blue Mist'** is a low-growing, mounding plant with fragrant, light blue flowers. **'Worcester Gold'** has bright, yellow-green foliage that contrasts vividly with the violet blue, late-summer flowers.

Bluebeard is cultivated for its aromatic stems, foliage and flowers.

Also called: bluebird, blue spirea **Features:** flowers, foliage, scent **Habit:** rounded, spreading, deciduous shrub **Height:** 24–36" (60–90 cm) **Spread:** 24"–6' (50 cm–1.8 m) **Hardiness:** zones 5–8

Boxwood

Buxus

Common boxwood (above & below)

Boxwoods are versatile evergreens. They can be pruned to form neat hedges, geometric shapes or fanciful creatures. When allowed to grow naturally, boxwoods form attractive, rounded mounds.

Growing

Boxwoods prefer to grow in **partial shade,** but they tolerate full sun if kept well watered. The soil should be **fertile, moist** and **well drained**. Mulching will benefit these shrubs.

Tips

These shrubs make excellent background plants in mixed borders.

Boxwood foliage contains **toxic** compounds that, when ingested, can cause severe digestive upset and possibly death.

Recommended

B. microphylla (littleleaf boxwood) is quite pest resistant and hardy to zones 6–8. The foliage tends to lose its green in winter. *B. m.* **var.** *koreana* is hardy to zone 4.

B. sempervirens (common boxwood) is a larger species with foliage that stays green in winter. Cultivars are available with interesting features such as compact or dwarf growth, variegated foliage and pendulous branches. (Zones 5–8)

Several cultivars developed from crossing *B. m.* **var.** *koreana* and *B. sempervirens* exhibit good hardiness and pest resistance, and have attractive year-round foliage. (Zones 4–8)

Also called: box **Features:** foliage; slow, even growth **Habit:** dense, rounded, evergreen shrub **Height:** 3–15' (1–4.5 m) **Spread:** equal to height **Hardiness:** zones 4–8

Butterfly Bush
Buddleia (Buddleja)

Orange eye butterfly bush (above & below)

Butterfly bushes can self-seed. You may find tiny bushes popping up in unlikely places around the garden.

Butterfly bushes are among the best shrubs for attracting butterflies and bees to a garden. Don't spray your bush for pests—you will harm its beautiful and beneficial insects.

Growing
Butterfly bushes prefer to grow in **full sun**. Plants grown in shade will produce few flowers. The soil should be **average to fertile** and **well drained**. These shrubs are drought tolerant once established.

Tips
Its graceful, arching branches make butterfly bush an excellent specimen plant and a beautiful addition to shrub and mixed borders.

To control this very fast-growing shrub, cut it back heavily in the spring, leaving just one-foot (30 cm) stumps. It will bloom that same summer.

Recommended
B. alternifolia (alternate-leaved butterfly bush) can be trained to form a small tree. In late spring or early summer, clusters of light purple flowers form on the ends of the branches. (Zones 4–8)

B. davidii (orange eye butterfly bush, summer lilac) bears flowers in bright and pastel shades of purple, white, pink or blue from mid-summer to fall. Many cultivars are available. (Zones 5–8)

Features: flowers, habit, foliage
Habit: deciduous large shrub or small tree with arching branches **Height:** 4–20' (1.2–6 m)
Spread: 4–20' (1.2–6 m)
Hardiness: zones 4–8

Camellia
Camellia

C. japonica (above), 'Buddha' (below)

Camellias tolerate salt and pollution, making them excellent choices for coastal and urban plantings.

Growing

Camellias prefer to grow in **light to partial shade** in **well-drained, acidic to neutral** soil high in organic matter. *C. japonica* prefers more acidic soil. Protect camellias from strong, hot sun and drying winds. They may also suffer damage if temperatures drop below 15° F (–10° C).

Plant so the base of the tree is slightly above grade and soil is not covering the base. Use organic mulch to help keep the roots cool for the first two to three years.

Tips

Camellias are evergreen plants suitable for mixed beds, borders and woodland gardens, as specimens or as container plants. The soil for container plantings should be 50% organic matter and 50% potting mix.

Recommended

There are almost 300 species of camellias and thousands of cultivars. Check with your local nursery or garden center to see what is available.

Features: flowers, foliage, habit **Habit:** upright to spreading shrub or small tree **Height:** 18"–20' (45 cm–6 m), sometimes to 50' (15 m) **Spread:** 3–12' (90 cm–3.5 m) **Hardiness:** zones: 7–9

Cedar

Cedrus

Deodar cedar (above), atlas cedar (below)

A portrait of Cedrus lebani *graces the national flag of Lebanon.*

A mature cedar tree, with its towering form and elegant, layered, sweeping branches, is truly a magnificent sight to behold. Do not confuse the 'true cedars' (*Cedrus*) with the native arborvitae (*Thuja*), which we commonly refer to as 'cedar.'

Growing

Cedars grow well in **full sun** or **partial shade.** The soil can be of any type as long as it is **well drained.** A **moist, loamy** soil of **average to high fertility** is preferable.

Tips

Cedars are very large trees, best suited to large properties and parks.

Recommended

C. atlantica (atlas cedar, blue atlas cedar) is a large, wide-spreading, pyramidal tree with branches that sweep the ground. Smaller cultivars are available. **'Glauca Pendula'** is an interesting cultivar with trailing branches. (Zones 6–8)

C. deodara (deodar cedar) is the largest and fastest growing cedar, but it is not very cold hardy. Cultivars more reasonable in size are often more tolerant of winter cold. (Zones 7–8)

C. lebani (cedar of Lebanon) is often too big for the home garden, but it has cultivars that suit space-restricted settings. (Zones 5–7)

Features: habit, foliage, cones, bark **Habit:** large, upright, spreading or pendulous, evergreen tree **Height:** 3–130' (1–40 m) **Spread:** 15–40' (4.5–12 m) **Hardiness:** zones 5–8

Cotoneaster

Cotoneaster

Bearberry cotoneaster (above & below)

Cotoneasters are tough, handsome, dependable, four-season shrubs. They are so versatile that they border on being overused.

Growing

Cotoneasters grow well in **full sun** or **partial shade**. The soil should be of **average fertility** and **well drained**.

Tips

Cotoneasters can be included in shrub or mixed borders. Low spreaders work well as groundcover, and shrubby species can be used to form hedges. Larger species are grown as small specimen trees and some low growers are grafted onto standards and grown as small, weeping trees.

Recommended

There are many cotoneasters to choose from. *C. adpressus* (creeping cotoneaster), *C. x 'Hessei'* and *C. horizontalis* (rockspray cotoneaster) are low-growing groundcover plants. *C. apiculatus* (cranberry cotoneaster) and *C. dammeri* (bearberry cotoneaster) are widespreading, low, shrubby plants. *C. salicifolius* (willowleaf cotoneaster) is an upright, shrubby plant that can be trained to form a small tree. These are just a few possibilities. Your local garden center will be able to help you find a suitable variety for your garden.

Features: foliage, early-summer flowers, persistent fruit, variety of forms **Habit:** evergreen or deciduous groundcover, shrub or small tree **Height:** 12"–15' (30 cm–4.5 m) **Spread:** 3–15' (1–4.5 m) **Hardiness:** zones 4–8

Dawn Redwood

Metasequoia

This tree is often called a 'living fossil' because it was discovered in fossil form before it was found growing in China in the 1940s. Dawn redwood is becoming a common sight in parks, golf courses and large gardens in North America.

Dawn redwood is a refined, pyramidal tree with attractive, deeply furrowed, cinnamon red, flaking bark. Don't worry when this ancient tree drops its needles—it's deciduous.

Growing
Dawn redwood grows well in **full sun** or **light shade.** The soil should be **humus rich,** slightly **acidic, moist** and **well drained.** It tolerates wet or dry soils, but growth rate is reduced in dry conditions. This tree likes humidity. Provide mulch and water regularly until it's established.

Tips
Dawn redwoods need plenty of room to grow. Large gardens and parks can best accommodate them.

The lower branches must be left in place in order for the trunk to develop its characteristic buttress. Buttressed trunks are flared and grooved, and the branches appear to be growing from deep inside the grooves.

Recommended
M. glyptostroboides has a pyramidal, sometimes spire-like form. The needles turn gold or orange in fall before dropping. The cultivars are narrower than the species.

Features: foliage, bark, cones, buttressed trunk
Habit: narrow, conical, deciduous conifer
Height: 70–125' (21–38 m) **Spread:** 15–25' (4.5–7.5 m)
Hardiness: zones 5–8

Dogwood

Cornus

Flowering dogwood (above & below)

The delicate branch patterns and spreading crowns of dogwood trees can add classic beauty to your garden.

Growing

Dogwoods grow equally well in **full sun, light shade** or **partial shade**, with a slight preference for light shade. The soil should be of **average to high fertility, high in organic matter, neutral or slightly acidic** and **well drained**.

Tips

Plant shrub dogwoods in groups in shrub or mixed borders. Tree species make wonderful specimens and are small enough to include in most gardens. Use them along the edge of a woodland garden, in a shrub or mixed border, alongside a house or near a pond, water feature or patio.

Recommended

There are numerous dogwoods available. Small shrub species and their cultivars are tough plants, often grown for their bright red, orange or yellow stems that provide winter interest. The larger shrubs and trees bear inconspicuous flowers surrounded by showy white or pink bracts in spring or early summer. Some species have attractive horizontal branching and some bear showy fruit. Many have attractive fall color. Check with your local garden center for availability.

C. kousa is more dependable and disease resistant than many other dogwood species.

Features: late-spring to early-summer flowers, fall foliage, stem color, fruit, habit **Habit:** deciduous shrub or small tree **Height:** 5–40' (1.5–12 m) **Spread:** 5–30' (1.5–9 m) **Hardiness:** zones 2–8

Douglas-Fir
Pseudotsuga

We are very lucky to have magnificent native trees like Douglas-fir. Not only can they be used as large specimens, but they can be planted as seedlings in the smallest of gardens, then cut for use as Christmas trees in the future. The soft needles persist longer on cut trees than needles of spruce and fir.

Growing
Douglas-fir prefers **full sun.** The soil should be of **average fertility, moist, acidic** and **well drained.** Pruning is generally not required.

Tips
The species can be grown as a single large specimen tree or part of a group of trees. Smaller cultivars can be grown as specimens in gardens or as part of shrub or mixed borders.

Recommended
P. menziesii is a massive, native tree that can reach great age and height. Several less imposing cultivars of Douglas-fir work well in small gardens.

Douglas-fir cones have unique three-pronged bracts that look like the hind feet and tails of tiny mice hiding inside.

Features: foliage, cones, habit
Habit: conical evergreen, becomes columnar with age **Height:** 6–200' (1.8–60 m) **Spread:** 6–25' (1.8–7.5 m)
Hardiness: zones 4–8

Euonymus

Euonymus

Burning bush (above), wintercreeper euonymus (below)

ew plants can match the stunning fall color of burning bush, a popular euonymous variety. It can be used in many different landscape situations, as can wintercreeper euonymus.

Growing

Euonymus species prefer **full sun** and tolerate light or partial shade. Soil of **average to rich fertility** is preferable, but any **moist, well-drained** soil will do.

Tips

E. alatus can be grown in a shrub or mixed border, as a specimen, in a naturalistic garden or as a hedge. Dwarf cultivars can be used to create informal hedges. Grow *E. fortunei* as a shrub in a border or as a hedge. It is an excellent substitute for the more demanding boxwood. The trailing habit also makes it useful as a groundcover or climber.

Recommended

E. alatus (burning bush, winged euonymus) is an attractive, open, mounding, deciduous shrub with corky ridges on the stems and branches and vivid red fall foliage. Cultivars are available.

E. fortunei (wintercreeper euonymus) is the parent plant of many attractive cultivars. It can be a prostrate, climbing or mounding evergreen, often with attractive, variegated foliage.

The name euonymus *means 'of good name,' an ironic translation given that all parts of these plants are poisonous and violently purgative.*

Features: foliage, corky stems (*E. alatus*), habit **Habit:** deciduous and evergreen shrub, small tree, groundcover or climber **Height:** 24"–20' (50 cm–6 m) **Spread:** 24"–20' (50 cm–6 m) **Hardiness:** zones 3–8

False Cypress
Chamaecyparis

'Mops' Sawara false cypress (above), Lawson false cypress (below)

Conifer shoppers have a marvelous selection of false cypresses that offer color, size, shape and growth habits not available in most other evergreens.

Growing

False cypresses prefer **full sun**. The soil should be **fertile, moist, neutral to acidic** and **well drained**. Alkaline soils are tolerated. In shaded areas, growth may be sparse or thin.

The oils in the foliage of false cypress may irritate sensitive skin.

Tips

Tree varieties are used as specimen plants and for hedging. The dwarf and slow-growing cultivars are used in borders and rock gardens and as bonsai. False cypress shrubs can be grown near the house or as evergreen specimens in large containers.

Recommended

There are several available species of false cypress and many cultivars. The scaly foliage comes in a drooping or strand form, in fan-like or feathery sprays and may be dark green, bright green or yellow. Plant forms vary too, from mounding or rounded to tall and pyramidal or narrow with pendulous branches. Check with your local garden center or nursery to see what is available.

Features: foliage, habit, cones **Habit:** narrow, pyramidal, evergreen tree or shrub
Height: 12"–150' (50 cm–45 m) **Spread:** 12"–65' (50 cm–20 m) **Hardiness:** zones 4–8

Fir
Abies

Many firs have adapted to cool, moist forests and thrive on acidic soils, making them ideal trees for our environment. Firs look great in areas that resemble the mountain environment from which many of them originated.

Growing
Firs usually prefer **full sun,** but they tolerate partial shade. The soil should be **rich, moist, neutral to acidic** and **well drained.** Firs prefer **shelter** from the wind, and generally don't tolerate urban pollution. *A. concolor* tolerates pollution, heat and drought better than other *Abies* species.

Tips
Firs make impressive specimen trees in large areas. Dwarf cultivars can be included in shrub borders or planted as specimens.

Recommended
A. balsamea (balsam fir) looks pyramidal when it's young but narrows as it ages. (Zones 3–6)

A. concolor (white fir) is a large, pyramidal to conic tree. The needles have a whitish coating, giving the tree a hazy blue appearance. Cultivars with even whiter needles are available. (Zones 3–7)

White fir 'Candicans' (above), balsam fir (below)

A. procera (noble fir) is a symmetrical, pyramidal tree when it's young, and develops a domed crown with age. It is the largest of all the firs. (Zones 5–6)

Features: foliage, cones **Habit:** narrow, pyramidal or columnar, evergreen tree **Height:** 24"–100' (50 cm–30 m) **Spread:** 3–30' (1–9 m) **Hardiness:** zones 3–7

Fothergilla
Fothergilla

Foliage is a key element in a well-planned garden. Fothergilla has lovely gray-green leaves that stand out against evergreens in a woodland garden. It also boasts fiery fall foliage, which along with fragrant flowers and interesting soft tan to brownish stems, gives fothergilla year-round appeal.

Growing

Fothergillas grow equally well in **full sun and partial shade**. Full sun will produce the most flowers and the best fall color. The soil should be of **average fertility, acidic, humus rich, moist** and **well drained**.

Tips

Fothergillas are attractive and useful in shrub or mixed borders, in woodland gardens and when combined with evergreen groundcover. Fothergillas look great paired with rhododendrons and azaleas.

Recommended

Cultivars are available for both species.

F. gardenii (dwarf fothergilla) is a bushy shrub that bears fragrant white flowers. The foliage turns yellow, orange and red in fall.

F. major (large fothergilla) is a larger, rounded shrub that bears fragrant white flowers. The autumn colors are yellow, orange and scarlet.

Large fothergilla (above & below)

Fothergilla's bottlebrush-shaped flowers have a delicate honey scent.

Features: spring flowers, scent, fall foliage
Habit: dense, rounded or bushy, deciduous shrub **Height:** 24"–10' (50 cm–3 m) **Spread:** 24"–10' (50 cm–3 m) **Hardiness:** zones 4–8

Fringe Tree

Chionanthus

White fringe tree (above & below)

Cold-hardy fringe trees adapt to a wide range of growing conditions. They are densely covered in silky white, honey-scented flowers that shimmer in the wind for a long period in early summer.

Growing

Fringe trees prefer **full sun**. They do best in soil that is **fertile, acidic, moist** and **well drained** but they will adapt to most soil conditions.

Tips

Fringe trees work well as specimen plants, as part of a border or beside a water feature. Plants flower at a very early age.

Fruit from the fringe tree will attract birds to the garden, but if a tree lacks both female and male flowers, it will not produce fruit.

Recommended

C. retusus (Chinese fringe tree) is a rounded, spreading shrub or small tree with deeply furrowed, peeling bark and erect, fragrant, white flower clusters. (Zones 5–8)

C. virginicus (white fringe tree) is a spreading, small tree or large shrub that bears drooping, fragrant, white flowers. (Zones 4–8)

Features: early-summer flowers, bark, habit
Habit: rounded or spreading, deciduous, large shrub or small tree **Height:** 10–25' (3–7.5 m)
Spread: 10–25' (3–7.5 m)
Hardiness: zones 4–8

Heather
Erica

Golden heather (above), 'Mediterranean Pink' (below)

Heathers come in so many forms with such varied flowering times that you can enjoy a textural tapestry of flowering heather in your garden almost all year.

Growing
Heathers prefer **full sun** but tolerate partial shade. The soil should be of **average fertility, acidic, moist** and **well drained.** Though heathers prefer acidic soils and enjoy having peat moss mixed into the substrate, they will tolerate alkaline soil. Do not overfertilize.

Tips
Heathers make excellent groundcovers and rock garden plants. They can be combined with other acid-loving plants in a shrub or mixed border.

Recommended
E. carnea and its many, more commonly available cultivars have flowers in several shades of pink, red, purple and white. Its foliage colors include yellow, orange, bronze and many shades of green.

E. x darleyensis 'Mediterranean Pink' is a common, mounding groundcover that bears rose lavender flowers.

Also called: spring heath, winter heath
Features: late-winter to mid-spring flowers, foliage, habit **Habit:** low, spreading, evergreen shrub **Height:** 6–12" (15–30 cm) **Spread:** 8–36" (20–90 cm) **Hardiness:** zones 5–7

Hemlock

Tsuga

Many people would agree that hemlocks are some of the most beautiful, graceful evergreen trees in the world. The movement, softness and agility of these trees make them easy to place in the landscape.

Growing

Hemlock generally grows well in any light from **full sun to full shade**. The soil should be **humus rich, moist** and **well drained**. Hemlock is drought sensitive and grows best in cool, moist conditions. It is also sensitive to air pollution and suffers salt damage, so keep hemlock away from roadways.

Tips

These elegant trees, with their delicate needles, work very well as specimen trees. They can also be trimmed to form a hedge. The smaller cultivars may be included in a shrub or mixed border.

Recommended

T. canadensis (eastern hemlock, Canadian hemlock) is a graceful, narrowly pyramidal tree. Many cultivars are available, including groundcover, pendulous and dwarf forms.

T. heterophylla (western hemlock) is a tall tree with a spire-like habit. It prefers a sheltered site and is very shade tolerant. (Zones 6–8)

With the continued popularity of water gardening, hemlock is in demand for its naturalizing effect on pondscapes.

'Jeddeloh' eastern hemlock (above), eastern hemlock (below)

Features: foliage, habit, cones **Habit:** pyramidal or columnar, evergreen tree or shrub
Height: 5–130' (1.5–40 m) **Spread:** 6–35' (1.8–10 m) **Hardiness:** zones 3–8

Hydrangea

Hydrangea

Bigleaf hydrangea (above & below)

Hydrangeas have many attractive qualities including showy flowers and glossy green leaves, some of which turn beautiful colors in fall.

Growing

Hydrangeas grow well in **full sun** or **partial shade**, and some species tolerate full shade. Shade or partial shade will reduce leaf and flower scorch in hotter regions. The soil should be of **average to high fertility, humus rich, moist** and **well drained**. These plants perform best in cool, moist conditions.

Tips

Use hydrangeas in shrub or mixed borders, as specimens or informal barriers and in containers. Climbing hydrangea can be trained up walls, pergolas and arbors.

Recommended

H. arborescens (smooth hydrangea) is a rounded shrub that flowers well even in shade. (Zones 3–8)

H. macrophylla (bigleaf hydrangea) is a rounded or mounding shrub. Many cultivars are available. (Zones 6–8)

H. paniculata (panicle hydrangea) is a large, spreading to upright shrub or small tree. **'Grandiflora'** (peegee hydrangea) is commonly available. (Zones 4–8)

H. quercifolia (oakleaf hydrangea) is a mound-forming shrub with attractive, exfoliating bark and large, oak-like leaves. (Zones 4–8)

Features: flowers, habit, foliage, bark **Habit:** deciduous, mounding or spreading shrub or tree **Height:** 3–80' (1–24 m) **Spread:** 24"–20' (50 cm–6 m) **Hardiness:** zones 4–8

Italian Cypress
Cupressus

*I*talian cypresses are wonderful trees that work well as hedges and screens.

Growing

Italian cypress prefers **full sun, well-drained soil** and **shelter** from cold wind, but does well in heat and drier soil. Most Italian cypresses require little or no water after the second year.

Italian cypress doesn't usually require pruning. If growing Italian cypress as a hedge, begin training when the plant is young and only trim the young growth. Remove shoots that veer off in the wrong direction.

Tips

All Italian cypress are long lived and make excellent specimen trees. They are also used as screens, windbreaks, hedges and boulevard trees.

Recommended

C. sempervirens (Italian cypress) is either narrowly columnar with upright branches or conical with horizontal branches. Both forms grow to 70' (21 m) tall and the horizontal branching form spreads to 20' (6 m). Both bear dense sprays of gray-green to dark green foliage. TINY TOWER ('Monshelby') is a unique, compact form with very dense foliage that grows 8' (2.5 m) tall and 2' (60 cm) wide in 10 years. Mature size is estimated at 25–30' (7.5–9 m) tall and 6–8' (1.8–2.4 m) wide.

A unique feature of cypress is the mature bark that often breaks off into curling or rounded scales.

Italian cypress (right)

Also called: Mediterranean cypress, funeral cypress **Features:** foliage, habit, bark, cones
Habit: columnar to pyramidal, coniferous tree
Height: 20–70' (6–21 m) **Spread:** 3–20' (1–6 m)
Hardiness: zones 7–10

Japanese Kerria
Kerria

Kerria works very well as a rambling, understory shrub in a woodland garden or as a pruned specimen in a shrub border. Bright yellow, spring-blooming flowers, yellow fall foliage and distinctive yellow-green to bright green, arching stems make Japanese kerria an excellent addition to a garden.

Growing

Japanese kerria prefers **light shade, partial shade** or **full shade.** The soil should be of **average fertility** and **well drained.** Soil that is too fertile will produce a plant with few flowers.

Tips

Try planting Japanese kerria in group plantings, woodland gardens and shrub or mixed borders. Sporadic flowers may appear in summer.

Recommended

K. japonica has single yellow flowers. Cultivars are available with variegated foliage, double yellow flowers and white to light yellow flowers.

Features: mid- to late-spring flowers, habit
Habit: suckering, mounding, deciduous shrub
Height: 3–10' (1–3 m) **Spread:** 4–10' (1.2–3 m)
Hardiness: zones 4–8

Juniper
Juniperus

*J*unipers are tough and versatile. A form, color and texture is available for most landscaping situations.

Growing

Junipers prefer **full sun** but tolerate light shade. The soil should be of **average fertility** and **well drained**, but these plants tolerate most conditions.

Tips

Junipers make prickly barriers, hedges and windbreaks. They can be used in borders, as specimens or in groups. The low-growing species can be used in rock gardens and as groundcover. For interesting evergreen color, mix the yellow-foliaged junipers with those varieties with blue needles.

Recommended

Junipers vary from species to species and often from cultivar to cultivar within a species. *J. chinensis* (Chinese juniper) is a conical tree or spreading shrub. *J. conferta* (shore juniper) is a bushy, prostrate shrub. *J. horizontalis* (creeping juniper) is a prostrate, creeping groundcover. *J. procumbens* (Japanese garden juniper) is a wide-spreading, low shrub. *J. sabina* (savin juniper) is a spreading to erect shrub. *J. scopulorum* (Rocky Mountain juniper) can be upright, rounded, weeping or spreading. *J. squamata* (singleseed juniper) forms a prostrate or low, spreading shrub or a small, upright tree.

Singleseed juniper (above), 'Emerald Sea' shore juniper (below)

The prickly foliage may give some gardeners a rash.

Features: foliage; variety of color, size and habit **Habit:** conical or columnar tree, rounded or spreading shrub, prostrate groundcover, evergreen **Height:** 6"–70' (15 cm–21 m) **Spread:** 12"–25' (30 cm–7.5 m) **Hardiness:** zones 3–8

Katsura-Tree
Cercidiphyllum

'Pendula' (above), *C. japonicum* (below)

This tree is native to eastern Asia, and the delicate foliage blends well into Japanese-style gardens.

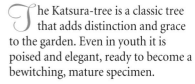

The Katsura-tree is a classic tree that adds distinction and grace to the garden. Even in youth it is poised and elegant, ready to become a bewitching, mature specimen.

Growing
Katsura-tree grows equally well in **full sun** or **partial shade**. The soil should be **fertile, humus rich, neutral to acidic, moist** and **well drained**. This tree will become established more quickly if watered regularly during dry spells for the first year or two.

Tips
Katsura-tree works well as a specimen or shade tree. The species is quite large and is best used in large gardens. The cultivar 'Pendula' is quite wide spreading but can be used in smaller gardens.

Recommended
C. japonicum is a slow-growing tree with heart-shaped, blue-green foliage that turns yellow and orange in fall and develops a spicy scent. **'Pendula,'** one of the most elegant weeping trees available, is usually grafted to a standard. Its mounding, cascading branches give the entire tree the appearance of a waterfall tumbling over rocks.

Features: summer and fall foliage, habit
Habit: rounded or spreading, often multi-stemmed, deciduous tree **Height:** 10–70' (3–21 m) **Spread:** 10–70' (3–21 m)
Hardiness: zones 4–8

Lilac
Syringa

Meyer lilac (above), French lilac (below)

The hardest thing about growing lilacs is choosing from the many species and hundreds of cultivars available.

Growing

Lilacs grow best in **full sun**. The soil should be **fertile, humus rich** and **well drained**. These plants tolerate open, windy locations.

Tips

Include lilacs in a shrub or mixed border, or use them to create an informal hedge. Japanese tree lilac can be used as a specimen tree.

Recommended

The following is a severely shortened list of really good lilacs. Check with your garden center to see what is available.

S. meyeri (Meyer lilac) is a compact, rounded shrub that bears fragrant pink or lavender flowers. (Zones 3–7)

S. microphylla (littleleaf lilac) is an upright, broad-spreading shrub with small, tidy leaves and attractive, airy clusters of fragrant, lilac pink flowers. (Zones 4–8)

S. patula (Manchurian lilac) is a hardy lilac with few suckers and small clusters of fragrant, lilac-colored flowers. **'Miss Kim'** is denser in habit. Its dark green leaves turn burgundy in fall. (Zones 3–8)

S. vulgaris (French lilac, common lilac) is a suckering, spreading shrub with an irregular habit and fragrant, lilac-colored flowers. (Zones 3–8)

Features: late-spring to mid-summer flowers, habit **Habit:** rounded or suckering, deciduous shrub or small tree **Height:** 4–20' (1.2–6 m) **Spread:** 4–20' (1.2–6 m) **Hardiness:** zones 3–8

Magnolia
Magnolia

Saucer magnolia (above & below)

agnolias are beautiful, fragrant, versatile plants that also provide attractive winter structure.

Growing

Magnolias grow well in **full sun** or **partial shade**. The soil should be **fertile, humus rich, acidic, moist** and **well drained**. A summer mulch will help keep the roots cool and the soil moist.

Tips

Magnolias are used as specimen trees and the smaller species can be used in borders.

Avoid planting magnolias where the morning sun will encourage the blooms to open too early in the season. Cold, wind and rain can damage the blossoms.

Recommended

Many species, hybrids and cultivars, in a range of sizes and with differing flowering times and flower colors, are available. The evergreen **M. grandiflora** (southern magnolia) is a large, dense, broad, pyramidal tree. Its spectacular, fragrant blooms have inspired poets and artists for generations. **M. x soulangeana** (saucer magnolia) is a rounded, spreading, deciduous shrub or tree with pink, purple or white flowers. **M. stellata** (star magnolia) is a compact, bushy or spreading, deciduous shrub or small tree with many-petaled, fragrant white flowers. Check with your local nursery or garden center for other available magnolias.

Features: flowers, fruit, foliage, habit, bark
Habit: upright to spreading, deciduous shrub or tree **Height:** 10–60' (3–18 m) **Spread:** 10–50' (3–15 m) **Hardiness:** zones 3–8

Maple

Acer

Maples are attractive all year, with delicate flowers in spring, beautiful foliage and hanging samaras in summer, vibrant leaf color in fall and interesting bark and branch structures in winter.

Growing

Generally, maples do well in **full sun** or **light shade,** though this varies from species to species. The soil should be **fertile, moist, high in organic matter** and **well drained**.

Tips

Use maples as specimen, shade or street trees, as large elements in shrub or mixed borders or as hedges. Some are useful as understory plants bordering wooded areas; others can be grown in containers on patios or terraces. A Japanese garden is not complete without attractive smaller maples. Almost all maples can be used to create bonsai specimens.

Recommended

Many maples grow very large, but smaller species that suit small gardens exist, including *A. circinatum* (vine maple, Oregon vine maple), *A. ginnala* (amur maple), *A. japonicum* (fullmoon maple, Japanese maple), *A. palmatum* (Japanese maple) and *A. rubrum* (red maple). Check with your local nursery or garden center for availability.

Japanese maple (above & below)

Features: foliage, bark, winged fruit (samaras), fall color, form, flowers **Habit:** small, multi-stemmed, deciduous tree or large shrub **Height:** 6–50' (1.8–15 m) **Spread:** 10–40' (3–12 m) **Hardiness:** zones 2–8

Pieris
Pieris

Need a shrub that doesn't lose its leaves or need pruning, blooms through spring and rarely has pest problems? *Pieris japonica* fits the bill and adds fragrance to the garden as a bonus.

Growing
Pieris grows equally well in **full sun** and **partial shade.** The soil should be of **average fertility, acidic, humus rich, moist** and **well drained.** Gardeners not in mild, coastal areas should ensure it has a sheltered location protected from the hot sun and drying winds.

Tips
Pieris can be used in a shrub or mixed border, in a woodland garden or as a specimen. Try grouping it with rhododendrons and other acid-loving plants.

Recommended
P. japonica bears white flowers in long, pendulous clusters at the ends of its branches. Several dwarf cultivars are available, as are cultivars with bright red new foliage, variegated foliage, and pink flowers.

'Mountain Fire' (above), *P. japonica* (below)

Pieris' flower buds form in late summer the year before the plant flowers, and they provide an attractive show all winter.

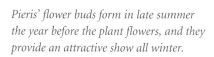

Also called: lily-of-the-valley shrub
Features: colorful new growth, late-winter to spring flowers **Habit:** compact, rounded, ever-green shrub **Height:** 3–12' (1–3.5 m)
Spread: 3–10' (1–3 m) **Hardiness:** zones 5–8

Pine
Pinus

Mugo pine (above), eastern white pine (below)

Pines offer exciting possibilities for any garden. Exotic-looking pines are available with soft or stiff needles, needles with yellow bands, trunks with patterned or mother-of-pearl-like bark and varied forms.

Growing

Pines grow best in **full sun**. These trees adapt to most **well-drained** soils but do not tolerate polluted urban conditions.

Tips

Pines can be used as specimen trees, as hedges or to create windbreaks. Smaller cultivars can be included in shrub or mixed borders. These trees are not heavy feeders; fertilizing will encourage rapid new growth that is weak and susceptible to pest and disease problems.

To keep low-growing pines compact, pinch up to half of the new growth each spring.

Recommended

There are many available pines, both trees and shrubby dwarf plants. Check with your local garden center or nursery to find out what is available.

Features: foliage, bark, cones, habit **Habit:** upright, columnar or spreading, evergreen trees **Height:** 8–130' (2.5–40 m) **Spread:** 15–60' (4.5–18 m) **Hardiness:** zones 2–8

Potentilla
Potentilla

'Tangerine' (above & below)

Potentilla is a fuss-free shrub that blooms madly all summer. The cheery, yellow-flowered variety is often seen, but cultivars with flowers in shades of pink, red and tangerine have increased this reliable shrub's popularity.

Growing
Potentilla prefers **full sun** but will tolerate partial or light shade. The soil should be of **poor to average fertility** and **well drained**. This plant tolerates most conditions, including sandy or clay soil and wet or dry conditions. Established plants are drought tolerant. Too much fertilizer or too rich a soil will encourage weak, floppy, disease-prone growth.

Tips
Use potentilla in shrub or mixed borders, on steep slopes that are awkward to mow, or as a low, informal hedge. Smaller cultivars can be included in rock gardens and on rock walls.

Recommended
P. fruticosa has many popular and interesting cultivars. **'Abbotswood'** is one of the best white-flowered cultivars, **'Pink Beauty'** bears pink semi-double flowers, **'Tangerine'** has orange flowers and **'Yellow Gem'** has bright yellow flowers.

Also called: shrubby cinquefoil **Features:** flowers, foliage, habit **Habit:** mounding, deciduous shrub **Height:** 12–48" (30 cm–1.2 m) **Spread:** 12–48" (30 cm–1.2 m) **Hardiness:** zones 2–8

Rhododendron • Azalea

Rhododendron

We are blessed to be able to grow many exceptional rhododendrons and azaleas. Visitors from central North America gush over the huge, abundant, colorful blossoms and equally photogenic leaves.

Growing

Rhododendrons prefer **partial shade** or **light shade,** but they tolerate full sun in a site with adequate moisture. A location sheltered from strong winds is preferable. The soil should be **fertile, humus rich, acidic, moist** and **very well drained.** Rhododendrons are sensitive to high pH, salinity and winter injury.

Tips

Use rhododendrons and azaleas in shrub or mixed borders, in woodland gardens, as specimen plants, in group plantings, as hedges and informal barriers, in rock gardens or in planters on a shady patio or balcony.

Rhododendrons and azaleas are generally grouped together. Extensive breeding and hybridizing makes it more and more difficult to label them separately.

Recommended

In our area, we can grow many different rhododendron and azalea species and cultivars. Many wonderful nurseries and specialty growers can help you find the right rhododendron or azalea for your garden.

Evergreen rhododendron (above), Exbury azalea (below)

Weevils often make notches along the leaf margins of rhododendrons. The variety 'PJM' is resistant to these insects.

Features: late-winter to early-summer flowers, foliage, habit **Habit:** upright, mounding, rounded, evergreen or deciduous shrub **Height:** 24"–12' (50 cm–3.5 m) **Spread:** 24"–12' (50 cm–3.5 m) **Hardiness:** zones 3–8

Smokebush
Cotinus

'Royal Purple' (above & below)

Try encouraging a clematis vine to wind its way through the spreading branches of a smokebush.

Bright fall color, adaptability, flowers of differing colors and variable plant sizes and forms make smokebush and all its cultivars excellent additions to the garden.

Growing
Smokebush grows well in **full sun** or **partial shade**. It prefers soil of **average fertility** that is **well drained**, but it will adapt to all but very wet soils.

Tips
Smokebush can be used in a shrub or mixed border, as a single specimen or in groups. It is a good choice for a rocky hillside planting.

Recommended
C. coggygria is a bushy, rounded shrub with large, puffy plumes of flowers that start out green and gradually turn a pinky gray. The green foliage turns red, orange and yellow in fall. Many cultivars are available, including purple-leaved varieties. **'Flame'** develops into a small, bushy tree or large shrub with purple-pink plumes and brilliant red fall color. **'Royal Purple'** has dark purple foliage and purple-gray flowers.

Also called: smoketree
Features: early-summer flowers, summer and fall foliage **Habit:** bushy, rounded, spreading, deciduous tree or shrub **Height:** 10–20' (3–6 m)
Spread: 10–15' (3–4.5 m)
Hardiness: zones 4–8

Spirea

Spiraea

Bridal wreath spirea (above & below)

Spireas, seen in so many gardens and with dozens of cultivars, remain undeniable favorites. With a wide range of forms, sizes and colors of both foliage and flowers, spireas have many landscape uses.

Growing

Spireas prefer **full sun**. To help prevent foliage burn, provide protection from very hot sun. The soil should be **fertile, acidic** and **well drained**.

Tips

Spireas are used in shrub or mixed borders, in rock gardens and as informal screens and hedges.

Recommended

Many species and cultivars of spirea are available. Three popular hybrid groups

include: **S. x *bumalda*** (*S. japonica* 'Bumalda') is a low, broad, mounded shrub with pink flowers. It is rarely grown in favor of the many cultivars, which have pink flowers and brightly colored foliage. **S. *japonica*** (Japanese spirea) forms a clump of erect stems and bears pink or white flowers. **S. x *vanhouttei*** (bridal wreath spirea, Vanhoutte spirea) is a dense, bushy shrub with arching branches that bears clusters of white flowers. Check at your local nursery or garden center to see what is available.

This shrub is part of the rose family; under a magnifying glass its flowers do indeed resemble tiny roses.

Features: summer flowers, habit **Habit:** round, bushy, deciduous shrub **Height:** 12"–10' (30 cm–3 m) **Spread:** 12"–12' (30 cm–3.5 m) **Hardiness:** zones 3–8

Spruce
Picea

Dwarf white spruce cultivar (above), 'Moerheim' Colorado blue spruce (below)

he spruce is one of the most commonly grown and commonly abused evergreens. Plant spruces where they have enough room to spread, then let them branch all the way to the ground.

Growing

Spruce trees grow best in **full sun**. The soil should be **deep, moist, well drained** and **neutral to acidic**. These trees generally do not like hot, dry or polluted conditions. Spruces are best grown from small, young stock as they dislike being transplanted after they mature.

Oil-based pesticides such as dormant oil can take the blue out of your blue-needled spruces.

Tips

Spruces are used as specimen trees. The dwarf and slow-growing cultivars can also be used in shrub or mixed borders. These trees look most attractive when allowed to keep their lower branches.

Recommended

Spruce are generally upright, pyramidal trees, but cultivars may be low growing, wide spreading or even weeping in habit. *P. abies* (Norway spruce), *P. breweriana* (weeping spruce, Brewer spruce), *P. glauca* (white spruce), *P. omorika* (Serbian spruce), *P. pungens* (Colorado spruce) and their cultivars are popular and commonly available. The most common spruce for home landscaping is the cone-shaped *P. glauca* var. *albertiana* **'Conica'** (dwarf Alberta spruce), a slow-growing specimen shrub.

Features: foliage, cones, habit **Habit:** conical or columnar, evergreen tree or shrub **Height:** 3–80' (1–25 m) **Spread:** 3–25' (60 cm–7.5 m) **Hardiness:** zones 2–8

Stewartia
Stewartia

Stewartias are wonderful plants that provide year-round interest. Plant them in areas such as the front yard or near a patio where their large, white, summer blooms, brilliant fall color and exfoliating bark, which peels or flakes, will be most appreciated.

Growing

Stewartias grow well in **full sun** or **light shade.** The soil should be of **average to high fertility, humus rich, neutral to acidic, moist** and **well drained.** These plants need some **shelter** from strong winds. Plant only very young trees as they do not transplant easily.

Tips

Plant stewartias as specimen trees and in groups. They make good companions for rhododendrons and azaleas because they enjoy the same growing conditions.

Recommended

S. monadelpha (tall stewartia) can be a shrubby and multi-stemmed or narrowly conical and single-stemmed tree.

S. pseudocamellia (Japanese stewartia) is a broad, columnar or pyramidal tree.

Tall stewartia (above & below)

Don't be concerned if the bark doesn't put on a display when you first plant a stewartia. It can take several years for the bark to flake. Branches less than 2" (5 cm) in diameter don't exfoliate.

Features: mid-summer flowers, summer and fall foliage, exfoliating bark **Habit:** broad, conical or rounded, deciduous tree **Height:** 20–80' (6–25 m) **Spread:** 20–40' (6–12 m) **Hardiness:** zones 5–8

Viburnum
Viburnum

Doublefile viburnum (above & below)

Good fall color, attractive form, shade tolerance, scented flowers and attractive fruit put the viburnums in a class by themselves.

Growing
Viburnums grow well in **full sun, partial shade** or **light shade**. The soil should be of **average fertility, moist** and **well drained**. Viburnums tolerate both alkaline and acidic soils.

Tips
Viburnums can be used in borders and woodland gardens. They are a good choice for plantings near swimming pools.

Recommended
Many viburnum species, hybrids and cultivars are available. Hardiness varies among species. Some popular choices include *V. carlesii* (Korean spice viburnum), a dense, bushy, rounded, deciduous shrub with white or pink spicy-scented flowers; *V. plicatum* var. *tomentosum* (doublefile viburnum), with lacy-looking white flower clusters and graceful, horizontal branches that give the shrub a layered effect; *V. trilobum* (American cranberry-bush, highbush cranberry), a dense, rounded shrub with clusters of white flowers followed by edible red fruit; and *V. tinus* '**Spring Bouquet,**' a dense, compact shrub with clusters of white flowers and persistent blue fruit that ripens to black.

Features: flowers (some fragrant), summer and fall foliage, fruit **Habit:** bushy or spreading, evergreen, semi-evergreen or deciduous shrub **Height:** 2–15' (50 cm–4.5 m) **Spread:** 2–15' (50 cm–4.5 m) **Hardiness:** zones 2–8

Weigela
Weigela

Weigelas have been improved through breeding, and specimens with more compact forms, longer flowering periods and greater cold tolerance are now available.

Growing

Weigelas prefer **full sun** but tolerate partial shade. The soil should be **fertile** and **well drained**. These plants will adapt to most well-drained soil conditions.

Tips

Weigelas can be used in shrub or mixed borders, in open woodland gardens and as informal barrier plantings.

Recommended

W. florida is a spreading shrub with arching branches that bears clusters of dark pink flowers. Many hybrids and cultivars are available, including dwarf varieties, red-, pink- or white-flowered varieties and varieties with purple, bronze or yellow foliage. The following are some newer selections: FRENCH LACE ('Brigela') has lime green to yellow leaf margins and dark, reddish pink flowers. MIDNIGHT WINE ('Elvera') is a dwarf plant with purple foliage and pink flowers. WINE AND ROSES ('Alexandra') has dark purple foliage and vivid pink flowers.

'Polka' (above),
'Siebold Variegata' (middle)

Weigela is one of the longest-blooming shrubs, with its main flush of blooms lasting as long as six weeks. It often re-blooms if sheared lightly after the first flowers fade.

W. florida (below)

Features: late-spring to early-summer flowers, foliage, habit **Habit:** upright or low, spreading, deciduous shrub
Height: 12"–9' (30 cm–2.7 m)
Spread: 12"–12' (30 cm–3.5 m)
Hardiness: zones 3–8

Witch-Hazel

Hamamelis

Common witch-hazel (above & below)

Witch-hazels are wonderful four-season plants. They bloom in mid- to late winter, the flowers last for weeks and their spicy fragrance awakens the senses.

Growing

Witch-hazel grows best in a sheltered spot with **full sun** or **light shade**. The soil should be of **average fertility, neutral to acidic, moist** and **well drained**.

Tips

Witch-hazels work well individually or in groups. Plant them as specimen plants, in shrub or mixed borders or in woodland gardens. As small trees, they are ideal for small gardens.

Recommended

H. x *intermedia* is a vase-shaped, spreading shrub that bears yellow, orange or red flowers and provides orange, red and bronze fall color.

H. japonica (Japanese witch-hazel) is an open, wide-spreading tree with yellow flowers, yellow fall color and attractive crisscrossed branches.

H. mollis (Chinese witch-hazel) is a dense, rounded, spreading shrub with zigzagged branches, very fragrant yellow flowers and orange or yellow fall color.

H. virginiana (common witch-hazel) is an erect tree with yellow fall foliage and flowers.

Features: fragrant, early-spring flowers; summer and fall foliage; habit **Habit:** spreading, deciduous shrub or small tree **Height:** 10–20' (3–6 m) **Spread:** 10–20' (3–6 m) **Hardiness:** zones 5–8

Yew

Taxus

Japanese yew (above), English Japanese yew (below)

From sweeping hedges to commanding specimens, yews can serve many purposes in the garden. They are one of the few reliable evergreens that grow in deep shade.

Growing

Yews grow well in any light conditions from **full sun to full shade**. The soil should be **fertile, moist** and **well drained**. These trees tolerate windy, dry and polluted conditions, and soils of any acidity. They dislike excessive heat, however, and on the hotter south or southwest side of a building they may suffer needle scorch.

Tips

Yews can be used in borders or as specimens, hedges, topiary and groundcover.

Recommended

T. cuspidata (Japanese yew) is a slow-growing, broad, columnar or conical tree. Dwarf cultivars are available.

T. x media (English Japanese yew), a cross between *T. baccata* (English yew) and *T. cuspidata* (Japanese yew), has the vigor of the English yew and the cold hardiness of the Japanese yew. It forms a rounded, upright tree or shrub, though the size and form can vary among the many cultivars.

Male and female flowers are borne on separate plants. Both must be present for the attractive red arils (seed cups) to form.

Features: foliage, habit, red seed cups
Habit: evergreen; conical or columnar tree or bushy or spreading shrub **Height:** 12"–7' (30 cm–21 m) **Spread:** 12"–30' (30 cm–9 m)
Hardiness: zones 4–8

Yucca
Yucca

'Golden Sword' in mixed planting (above), *Y. filamentosa* (below)

The striking white flowers are edible raw or cooked and are said to taste like Belgian endive. Try adding them to a salad.

Yucca will add a touch of the desert to your personal oasis.

Growing
Yucca grows best in **full sun**. Any **well-drained** soil is suitable. This drought-tolerant plant grows best in areas of low humidity.

Pruning is not needed, but the flower spikes can be removed when flowering is finished, and dead leaves can be removed as needed.

Tips
This spiky plant looks as though it belongs in a desert or a southern garden. As a specimen in pots, planters and urns, this plant makes a strong architectural statement. The variegated varieties add color and texture to beds and borders.

Recommended
Y. filamentosa has long, stiff, finely serrated, pointed leaves with threads that peel back from the edges. It is the most frost-hardy yucca species available. **'Bright Edge'** has leaves with yellow margins. **'Golden Sword'** has leaves with yellow centers and green margins. **'Hofer's Blue'** has attractive, blue-green leaves and is salt tolerant.

Also called: Adam's needle
Features: summer flowers, foliage, habit **Habit:** rounded rosette of long, stiff, spiky, evergreen leaves
Height: 24–36" (60–90 cm); up to 6' (1.8 m) in flower **Spread:** 24–36" (60–90 cm) **Hardiness:** zones 5–9

Bobbie James

Rambling Rose

Bobbie James' once-yearly bloom is a memorable sight. This rose bears thousands of semi-double, sweetly scented, cupped blooms in drooping clusters of 50 flowers or more.

Growing

Bobbie James prefers to grow in **full sun** and **fertile, moist, well-drained** soil with at least **5% organic matter** mixed in. It can tolerate light breezes, but keep it out of strong winds. Roses are heavy feeders and drinkers, and do not like to share their root space with other plants.

Tips

This giant rambler requires substantial support, and should be planted where it can reach its full mature height and spread. It can eventually grow to cover a three-car garage or an outbuilding. It looks very attractive when allowed to twine over an old, sturdy tree.

Recommended

Rosa **'Bobbie James'** produces long, thick, prickly stems and an abundance of glossy, deep green leaves with coppery edges.

Lone Pine author and BC resident Brad Jalbert has a seven-year-old Bobbie James rose that is approximately 40' (12 m) tall. Jalbert has never sprayed the plant for disease, fertilized or pruned it, and the healthy rose blooms prolifically.

Water all roses at the base rather than from above, and try to water early in the morning.

Features: profuse, non-repeating, mid-summer flowers; form; foliage
Flower color: creamy white with showy, golden stamens **Height:** 28–30' (8.5–9 m)
Spread: 20' (6 m) **Hardiness:** zones 5–9

Bonica

Modern Shrub Rose

Bonica was the first modern shrub rose to be named an All-America Selection. The blooms have a light and sweet fragrance. Bright orange hips appear after the pink, double flowers fade.

Growing

Bonica prefers **full sun** and **fertile, moist, well-drained** soil with at least **5% organic matter** mixed in. It can tolerate light breezes, but keep it out of strong winds. Roses are heavy feeders and drinkers, and do not like to share their root space with other plants. This disease-resistant, hardy rose tolerates shade and poor soils.

Tips

Bonica suits just about any location. Rose growers recommend it for mixed beds, containers, hedges, cut-flower gardens or as a groundcover, standard or specimen.

Recommended

Rosa 'Bonica' is a tidy, spreading rose of modest size that blooms profusely throughout most of the growing season. It bears an abundance of semi-glossy, rich green foliage that is beautiful enough to stand on its own.

Also called: Bonica '82, Meidomonac, Demon, Bonica Meidiland **Features:** repeat-blooming, summer to fall flowers; easy maintenance; colorful hips **Flower color:** medium pink **Height:** 3–5' (90 cm–1.5 m) **Spread:** 3–4' (90 cm–1.2 cm) **Hardiness:** zones 4–9

Chevy Chase

Rambling Rose

A good, red rambling rose is hard to find, and this one has grown in popularity. As one of the best overall ramblers for a coastal environment, Chevy Chase is in high demand.

Growing

Chevy Chase prefers **full sun** and **fertile, moist, well-drained** soil with at least **5% organic matter** mixed in. It can tolerate light breezes, but keep it out of strong winds. Roses are heavy feeders and drinkers, and do not like to share their root space with other plants. Chevy Chase is disease resistant but a little prone to rust.

It may require some pruning and dead-heading for best results.

Tips

Chevy Chase can be trained on a fence to create privacy, but the canes are quite stiff and difficult to work with. Its long-lasting blooms are ideal for cutting and arranging.

Recommended

Rosa **'Chevy Chase'** bears tight, full clusters of small, double, moderate- to strong-scented, crimson flowers, which create a good contrast with its light gray-green, wrinkled foliage. Hooked prickles cover the canes.

Once fully established, this vigorous plant reaches its mature height in one season.

Features: non-repeating, mid-summer flowers; vigorous growth **Flower color:** deep crimson red **Height:** 15' (4.5 m) **Spread:** 8' (2.4 m) **Hardiness:** zones 5–9

Double Delight
Hybrid Tea Rose

Double Delight is a long-lasting cut flower and a good choice for competition and exhibition.

Double Delight is aptly named; it delights with its strong, sweet, lightly spicy fragrance and its unique flower color. The fully double, high-centered flowers open cream with red edges and gradually darken to solid red. Heat intensifies the color.

Growing
Double Delight prefers **full sun** and **fertile, moist, well-drained** soil with at least **5% organic matter** mixed in. Roses can tolerate light breezes, but keep them out of strong winds. Double Delight is a heavy feeder and drinker, and it does not like to share its root space with other plants.

Blackspot can be a problem for Double Delight. Cool, wet weather can promote mildew.

Tips
It's hard to find a place for this unique flower color in a bed or border. Plant it in a warm, dry location or in a container where it can be monitored for disease.

Recommended
Rosa 'Double Delight' is an upright, irregularly branched plant with mid-green foliage. Its fragrance is unaffected by temperature, light or age.

Also called: Andeli **Features:** repeat blooming, summer to fall flowers; flower color; fragrance **Flower color:** cream with carmine red edges **Height:** 3–4' (90 cm–1.2 m) **Spread:** 24–36" (60–90 cm) **Hardiness:** zones 6–9

Flower Carpet

Modern Shrub Rose

Flower Carpet is popular and easy to grow for a beginner or an expert.

Growing

Flower Carpet prefers to grow in **full sun** in **fertile, moist, well-drained** soil with at least **5% organic matter** mixed in. Keep it out of strong winds, but light breezes are okay. Roses are heavy feeders and drinkers, and do not like to share their root space with other plants.

Tips

Flower Carpet can be used as a groundcover for a sunny location or as a low hedge. Plant it in containers, mixed borders or beds.

Recommended

Rosa 'Flower Carpet' is a vigorous, disease-resistant rose with abundant, shiny, bright green foliage. The flowers bloom later than most roses, and are borne in large clusters, creating a dense, colorful carpet of flowers. In mild coastal climates, it can hold its leaves through winter.

A new color of Flower Carpet has been introduced almost every year since its original release, including white, apple blossom, pink, red and coral.

Also called: Heidetraum, Noatraum, Emera, Blooming Carpet, Emera Pavement, Pink Flower Carpet **Features:** summer to early-winter, repeat-blooming flowers; easy to grow **Flower color:** white, apple blossom, pink, red, coral **Height:** 30–36" (75–90 cm) **Spread:** 3–4' (90 cm–1.2 m) **Hardiness:** zones 4–9

Fragrant Cloud
Hybrid Tea Rose

Fragrant Cloud has been showered with numerous honors and awards, most in recognition of its outstanding scent.

Although its full, bright, orangy red flowers are beautiful in their own right, Fragrant Cloud is best known for its outstanding, unique fragrance.

Growing
Fragrant Cloud prefers **full sun** and **fertile, moist, well-drained** soil with at least **5% organic matter** mixed in. Light breezes are tolerable, but keep roses out of strong winds. Roses are heavy feeders and drinkers, and do not like to share their root space with other plants.

Fragrant Cloud is only mildly prone to mildew in the fall and blackspot in damp weather.

Tips
Fragrant Cloud is ideal for borders and beds. It requires very little maintenance other than seasonal deadheading and a little spring pruning. Cool climates produce the best flower color.

Recommended
Rosa **'Fragrant Cloud'** is bushy and upright, with well-branched canes and glossy, dark green foliage. It bears typical, high-centered, double, hybrid tea flowers made up of more than 30 petals each.

Also called: Nuage Parfume
Features: repeat-blooming, summer to fall flowers; fragrance; size
Flower color: orangy red **Height:** 4–5' (1.2–1.5 m) **Spread:** 32–36" (80–90 cm) **Hardiness:** zones 5–9

Gourmet Popcorn
Miniature Rose

Gourmet Popcorn bears cascading clusters of rounded, white, semi-double, honey-scented flowers with short stems.

Growing
Gourmet Popcorn prefers **full sun** and **fertile, moist, well-drained** soil with at least **5% organic matter** mixed in. It can tolerate light breezes, but keep it out of strong winds. Roses are heavy feeders and drinkers, and do not like to share their root space with other plants.

Tips
Gourmet Popcorn looks stunning planted en masse or in pots, containers and hanging baskets. Plant this rose where its fragrance can be enjoyed—alongside pathways, under windows or next to a garden bench.

In warmer regions, Gourmet Popcorn can grow up to twice its typical height, creating an impressive specimen with hundreds of flowers in bloom at a time.

Recommended
Rosa '**Gourmet Popcorn**' is a vigorous, compact, cushion-like, rounded shrub with lush, dark green foliage. It is resistant to disease.

Also called: Summer Snow **Features:** form; repeat blooming; abundant, summer to fall flowers **Flower color:** white **Height:** 18–24" (45–60 cm) **Spread:** 24" (60 cm) **Hardiness:** zones 4–9

Hénri Martin

Old Garden Rose

Hénri Martin is known for its moss-covered stems and sepals that emit a subtle balsam scent. It bears clusters of camellia-like, semi-double to double, rich pinky red, sweetly fragrant blossoms that pale with age.

Growing

Hénri Martin grows well in **full sun** and tolerates light shade. Plant it in **fertile, moist, well-drained** soil with at least **5% organic matter** mixed in. Roses tolerate light breezes, but keep them out of strong winds. They are heavy feeders and drinkers, and do not like to share their root space with other plants.

Hénri Martin tolerates hot and dry summers and poor soil. It may suffer some winter dieback in colder regions. Prune out any deadwood in spring.

Tips

Hénri Martin's arching, flexible canes require support. It grows well on an obelisk, trellis, tripod or pergola.

Recommended

Rosa **'Hénri Martin'** is a vigorous moss rose with graceful, arching branches and plentiful, disease-free, rough foliage.

Attractive orangy red hips emerge after flowering and remain on the shrub well into winter.

Also called: Red Moss, Old Red Moss
Features: profuse, non-repeating, mid-summer flowers; colorful hips; fragrance; moss-covered stems and sepals **Flower color:** rich pinky red
Height: 3–5' (90 cm–1.5 m) **Spread:** 4' (1.2 m)
Hardiness: zones 4–9

Lavaglow
Floribunda Rose

*L*avaglow bears camellia-like, lightly scented flowers in a dark red hue that appears almost black. Each velvety blossom has an average of 20–25 petals. The evenly spaced clusters are well maintained through summer and fall.

Growing
Lavaglow prefers **full sun** and **fertile, moist, well-drained** soil with at least **5% organic matter** mixed in. Roses can tolerate light breezes, but keep them out of strong winds. Protection from blackspot may be required in areas that receive significant moisture.

Tips
Its balanced growth habit makes Lavaglow an outstanding bedding variety. Other uses include mixed borders or hedging.

Dark red roses often suffer from scorch in heat and wind, but Lavaglow's blooms are not adversely affected by hot sun, wind or rain.

Recommended
Rosa 'Lavaglow' is a compact, vigorous, upright plant with glossy, purplish green leaves that complement its long-lasting, ruffled flowers.

This rose received the Royal National Rose Society Trial Ground Certificate in 1980.

Also called: Lavaglut **Features:** repeat blooming, summer to fall flowers; form **Flower color:** dark red **Height:** 3–4' (90 cm–1.2 m) **Spread:** 24" (60 cm) **Hardiness:** zones 4–9

Mutabilis

Old Garden Rose

Mutabilis' vermilion buds give way to buff yellow flowers, which soon change from yellow into shades of pink and finally deep crimson. This changing color palette is an unusual but desirable trait that will brighten the gloomiest site.

Growing

Roses prefer to grow in **full sun** and **fertile, moist, well-drained** soil with at least **5% organic matter** mixed in. They are heavy feeders and drinkers, and do not like to share their root space with other plants. Mutabilis tolerates shade but is not fond of cold wind.

Tips

Mutabilis requires very little maintenance. It works best as a specimen, but makes a wonderful informal hedge. Its foliage contrasts well with the lighter foliage on other plants.

Recommended

Rosa '**Mutabilis**' has soft, red stems and glossy, red-tinged, dark green foliage. Plant size and shape will vary depending on its location. Some claim this rose can reach heights of 10–25' (3–7.5 m).

Also called: Tipo Idéale, *R. chinensis mutabilis,* *R. odorata* 'Mutabilis,' Butterfly Rose
Features: mid-summer, repeat-blooming flowers, disease-resistant foliage **Flower color:** yellow, then pink and crimson **Height:** 4–6' (1.2–1.8 m)
Spread: 3–5' (90 cm–1.5 m)
Hardiness: zones 5–10

Pat Austin

English (Austin) Rose

at Austin introduced a new and vivid color combination: rich copper shades on the uppersides of the petals and pale amber yellow on the undersides. It is difficult to miss this exceptional color contrast as the fragrant flowers open and expand.

Growing
Pat Austin prefers **full sun** and **fertile, moist, well-drained** soil with at least **5% organic matter** mixed in. Light breezes are tolerable, but keep roses out of strong winds. Roses are heavy feeders and drinkers, and do not like to share their root space with other plants.

Tips
Pat Austin blends beautifully into mixed shrub borders, informal beds or containers. It can also be trained as a short climber.

Recommended
Rosa 'Pat Austin' is a vigorous, medium-sized, gracefully spreading plant. The semi-glossy, deep green foliage complements the large, open, deeply cupped, coppery flowers. The flowers have a sharp, fruity fragrance.

Pat Austin may be difficult to find because it is such a recent introduction, but it is well worth looking for.

Features: repeat-blooming, summer to fall flowers; graceful form **Flower color:** coppery amber and yellow **Height:** 3' (90 cm) **Spread:** 4' (1.2 m) **Hardiness:** zones 5–9

Peace

Hybrid Tea Rose

Peace has a moderate level of disease resistance but is prone to blackspot in cooler climates. Its overall health has been compromised as a result of being cloned millions of times since its introduction in 1945.

In 1976, Peace was the first rose to be selected World's Favorite Rose by the World Federation of Rose Societies.

Growing

Peace prefers to grow in **full sun** in **fertile, moist, well-drained** soil with at least **5% organic matter** mixed in. Keep it out of strong winds, but light breezes are okay. Roses are heavy feeders and drinkers, and do not like to share their root space with other plants.

Tips

Peace is an ideal cut-flower variety. It is suitable for rose beds, hedges and borders, and is considered one of the best varieties to grow as a standard. It is a little resentful of hard pruning but fares well with moderate pruning.

Recommended

Rosa 'Peace' is an upright grower with moderately thorny canes bearing large, shiny, dark green foliage and mild, fruity scented flowers. The yellow flower color can become pale if the location is too hot, while the pink flower color intensifies in heat.

Also called: Gloria Dei, Mme. A. Meilland, Gioia, Beke, Fredsrosen **Features:** summer to fall, repeat-blooming flowers; easy to grow **Flower color:** soft yellow; baby pink edges **Height:** 4–6' (1.2–1.8 m) **Spread:** 3–4' (1–1.2 m) **Hardiness:** zones 5–9

Red-leafed Rose

Species Rose

Municipalities use this rose in open planting areas because it looks good and needs little care.

Growing

Red-leafed rose prefers to grow in **full sun** in **fertile, moist, well-drained** soil with at least **5% organic matter** mixed in. It is tolerant of less than ideal soil conditions. Red-leafed rose also tolerates shade but prefers full sun, which improves the depth of the foliage color. Keep it out of strong winds, but light breezes are okay. Most roses are heavy feeders and drinkers, and do not like to share their root space with other plants.

Tips

Red-leafed rose is ideal for use as a hedge because of its vigorous nature and arching, thorny, purple stems. It can also be used in shrub beds and borders. This rose thrives where most plants could not survive.

Recommended

Rosa glauca has starry, pink blossoms that make a striking contrast with the violet-tinted foliage. Clusters of small, rounded, dark red hips remain on the shrub well into the following spring.

Also called: *Rosa glauca (R. ferruginea, R. rubrifolia)*
Features: red-tinged foliage; early-summer, non-repeat blooming flowers; easy maintenance; tough **Flower color:** pink; white centers **Height:** 6' (1.8 m); up to 12' (3.7 m) with support **Spread:** 5–6' (1.5–1.8 m) **Hardiness:** zones 2–9

Royal Sunset
Climbing Rose

*I*ntense, apricot orange blossoms fade to a soft pink, tinged with apricot hues. The cupped, semi-double flowers, borne in clusters with a strong, fruity fragrance, bloom on new and old wood. Royal Sunset blooms profusely throughout summer well into fall.

Growing

Royal Sunset prefers **full sun** and **fertile, moist, well-drained** soil with at least **5% organic matter** mixed in. Roses can tolerate light breezes, but keep them out of strong winds. Roses are heavy feeders and drinkers, and do not like to share their root space with other plants.

Tips

Royal Sunset is best suited to growing against walls or fences. Or plant it in a large area where it can be fanned out onto a support.

Recommended

Rosa 'Royal Sunset' produces bushy, stiff growth and bears an abundance of dense, leathery, dark green foliage. The bronze and copper foliar highlights complement the bright, summery blossoms. The thick, reddish canes and attractive hips provide color well into winter.

Most apricot-colored climbers have a leggy growth habit, but Royal Sunset does not.

Features: repeat-blooming, mid-summer flowers; thick, colorful canes; attractive hips
Flower color: apricot pink with blended yellow
Height: 6–10' (1.8–3 m) **Spread:** 6' (1.8 m)
Hardiness: zones 5–10

Sandalwood

Miniature Rose

Sandalwood's russet or terra-cotta blooms have one of the most intriguing colors for a rose. The flower color looks best when grown in dappled or partial shade. The spicy-scented blossoms are very large compared to other miniatures.

Growing

Sandalwood prefers **full sun to light shade** and **fertile, moist, well-drained** soil with at least **5% organic matter** mixed in. It can tolerate light breezes, but keep it out of strong winds. Roses are heavy feeders and drinkers, and do not like to share their root space with other plants.

Winter coverage may be necessary. In late fall, protect the plant with an insulating layer of mulch.

Tips

Use Sandalwood in pots, containers, hanging baskets, beds and borders.

Recommended

Rosa '**Sandalwood**' is a small, mounding plant with glossy, dark green foliage that contrasts well with its flowers. It prefers adequate air circulation and is not particularly prone to any disease.

Brad Jalbert, Sandalwood's hybridizer, claims this rose is the most unusual and loved rose he has ever created.

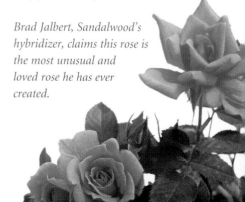

Features: repeat-blooming, early-summer to fall flowers; flower color **Flower color:** terra-cotta
Height: 14" (35 cm) **Spread:** 12" (30 cm)
Hardiness: zones 5–9

Sheila's Perfume

Floribunda Rose

Sheila's Perfume's showy, bicolored blooms have won several fragrance awards, including the Edland Fragrance Award and the Glasgow Fragrance Award. An average of 20 petals, borne singly or in clusters, makes up each double flower.

Growing

Sheila's Perfume prefers **full sun** in **fertile, moist, well-drained** soil with at least **5% organic matter** mixed in. Roses can tolerate light breezes, but keep them out of strong winds. Roses are heavy feeders and drinkers, and do not like to share their root space with other plants.

Tips

Sheila's Perfume bears a classically formed flower, making this plant ideal for cutting gardens, borders, hedges, mixed beds and containers.

Recommended

Rosa **'Sheila's Perfume'** is a compact, bushy plant that tends to spread throughout summer in warmer climates. It is vigorous, disease resistant and weatherproof, and has red-tinged, glossy, dark green foliage and fruit-scented flowers.

The name Sheila's Perfume reflects a combination of the hybridizer's wife's name and the plant's most outstanding quality.

Features: repeat-blooming, summer to fall, fragrant flowers **Flower color:** pale yellow and light pink with dark pink edges **Height:** 30–42" (75–105 cm) **Spread:** 24" (60 cm) **Hardiness:** zones 5–11

The Fairy
Modern Shrub Rose

The Fairy is popular with novice and experienced gardeners. It bears large clusters of dainty, soft pink, rosette-shaped, double flowers.

Growing

The Fairy grows well in **full sun or partial shade,** in **fertile, moist, well-drained** soil with at least **5% organic matter** mixed in. It is prone to blackspot when planted in partial shade, but will still bloom. Roses can tolerate light breezes, but keep them out of strong winds. These heavy feeders and drinkers do not like to share their root space with other plants. The Fairy's flower color fades more slowly in partial shade.

Tips

This rose can be used in containers, as groundcovers, in mixed beds and borders, as a weeping standard, or left to trail over a low wall or embankment. It looks great massed or planted as low hedging. It also makes a beautiful cut flower.

Recommended

Rosa 'The Fairy' is a compact, mounding plant with moderately prickly canes and glossy foliage. It is trouble free and moderately resistant to disease. It blooms continually until fall frost.

Also called: Fairy, Feerie **Features:** repeat-blooming, late-summer to fall flowers; low maintenance **Flower color:** soft pink
Height: 24" (60 cm) **Spread:** 2–4' (60 cm–1.2 m)
Hardiness: zones 4–9

Tournament of Roses

Grandiflora Rose

Tournament of Roses' double, high-centered flowers are borne in symmetrical clusters of three to six. Each flower has 35 to 40 petals and a light, spicy fragrance.

Growing

Tournament of Roses prefers **full sun** and **fertile, moist, well-drained** soil with at least **5% organic matter** mixed in. It can tolerate light breezes, but keep it out of strong winds. Roses are heavy feeders and drinkers, and do not like to share their root space with other plants.

Tips

Tournament of Roses blends into mixed beds and borders, and works well in hedges and group plantings. This long-lasting cut flower is one of the best grandifloras for display and exhibition. Warm weather brings out the best flower color.

Recommended

Rosa **'Tournament of Roses'** is a moderately vigorous, upright plant with glossy, dark green foliage and abundant flowers in various shades of pink. It has excellent continuity of bloom.

Also called: Berkeley, Poesie **Features:** repeat-blooming, summer to fall, double flowers; easy to grow **Flower color:** medium coral pink **Height:** 36" (90 cm) **Spread:** 36" (90 cm) **Hardiness:** zones 4–9

Warm Welcome

Climbing Miniature Rose

arm Welcome is easy to grow and train, and is highly disease and weather resistant. Its clusters of small, slightly scented, semi-double, deep orange flowers contrast well with its foliage.

Growing

Warm Welcome prefers **full sun** and **fertile, moist, well-drained** soil with at least **5% organic matter** mixed in. Roses can tolerate light breezes, but not strong winds. As heavy feeders and drinkers, roses do not like to share their root space with other plants.

Tips

Warm Welcome can be trained to grow up walls, fences, trellises or pillars, but is most appropriate for confined spaces.

Blossoms cover Warm Welcome throughout the season. Attractive hips will form throughout fall into winter—do not deadhead.

Recommended

Rosa **'Warm Welcome'** produces upright, arching, stiff canes and dark, semi-glossy leaves. The foliage tends to darken with age, from a purple hue to a deep bronzy green.

Because its hybridizers managed to retain Warm Welcome's free-blooming habit, its creation was regarded as a hybridizing breakthrough.

Features: repeat-blooming, summer to fall flowers; attractive hips **Flower color:** orange with yellow centers **Height:** 7–8' (2.1–2.4 m) **Spread:** 7' (2.1 m) **Hardiness:** zones 4–9

Water Lily

Miniature Rose

ater Lily is a full-bodied, delicate-looking rose that bears creamy, pink-tinged flowers. The lightly scented flowers are very dense and rounded, and the tightly packed petals never fully open.

Growing

Water Lily prefers **full sun to partial shade** and **fertile, moist, well-drained** soil with at least **5% organic matter** mixed in. It can tolerate light breezes, but keep it out of strong winds. Roses are heavy feeders and drinkers, and do not like to share their root space with other plants.

Tips

Plant Water Lily in pots, containers, hanging baskets, beds and borders. The blooms last a long time and make excellent cut flowers. The flowers look stunning in classic arrangements or floating in rose bowls.

Recommended

Rosa 'Water Lily' is a dense, low maintenance plant. It sometimes bears up to 50 flowers on one stem. This easy-to-grow rose requires little care, only admiration. The densely packed foliage is impervious to disease or bad weather.

This is the perfect rose for wedding boutonnieres and small tussie mussies.

Features: repeat-blooming, summer to fall flowers; easy to grow
Flower color: cream with pink
Height: 24" (60 cm) **Spread:** 18" (45 cm) **Hardiness:** zones 4–9

Akebia
Akebia

A. quinata (above & below)

This vigorous vine will twine up anything that gets in its way. It can become invasive, so keep the pruning shears handy if you plan to sit near it. It can be evergreen near the coast, especially when planted close to a house.

Growing
Akebia grows equally well in **full sun, light shade** or **partial shade** in **well-drained** soil of **average to high fertility**. It tolerates dry or moist soils and full shade.

Tips
Though the flowers and fruit of this vine are interesting, it is worth growing for the foliage alone. Akebia will quickly cover any sturdy structure such as a porch railing, trellis, pergola, arbor or fence. Cut the plant back as much and as often as needed to keep it under control.

Recommended
A. quinata is a fast-growing, twining, deciduous climbing vine. The new foliage is tinged purple in the spring and matures to blue-green. Deep purple flowers are borne in spring followed by sausage-like fruit pods. **'Alba'** bears white flowers and

This vine can quickly provide privacy and shade when grown over a chain-link fence or on a trellis next to a porch.

Also called: fiveleaf akebia **Features:** foliage, habit, flowers, fruit **Flower color:** purple, white **Height:** 20–40' (6–12 m) **Spread:** 20–40' (6–12 m) **Hardiness:** zones 4–8

Black-Eyed Susan Vine
Thunbergia

T. alata (above & below)

The blooms are actually trumpet shaped, with the dark centers forming a tube.

Black-eyed Susan vine is a useful flowering vine with simple flowers that give it a cheerful, welcoming appearance.

Growing
Black-eyed Susan vines do well in **full sun**, **partial shade** or **light shade**. Grow in **fertile, moist, well-drained** soil that is high in **organic matter**.

Tips
Black-eyed Susan vines can be trained to twine up and around fences, walls, trees and shrubs. They also look attractive trailing down from the top of a rock garden or rock wall or growing in mixed containers and hanging baskets.

Recommended
T. alata is a vigorous, twining climber. It bears yellow flowers, often with dark centers, in summer and fall. Cultivars with large flowers in yellow, orange or white are available.

T. grandiflora (skyflower vine, blue trumpet vine) is less commonly available than *T. alata*. It tends to bloom late, in early to mid-fall. This twining climber bears stunning, pale violet blue flowers. **'Alba'** has white flowers.

Features: twining habit; dark-centered flowers **Flower color:** yellow, orange, violet blue, creamy white **Height:** 5' (1.5 m) or more **Spread:** 5' (1.5 m) or more **Hardiness:** tender perennial treated as an annual

Clematis

Clematis

Clematis loves to grow up stumps where its roots can feed on decaying stump roots. Planted on the north side of a stump, this perennial vine will clamber to the sunny side.

Growing

Clematis plants prefer **full sun** but tolerate partial shade. The soil should be **fertile, humus rich, moist** and **well drained**. These vines prefer their roots to be cool. A thick layer of mulch or a planting of low, shade-providing perennials will protect the tender roots. Clematis are quite cold hardy but will fare best when protected from winter wind. The rootball should be planted about 2" (5 cm) beneath the soil surface.

Tips

Clematis vines climb up structures such as trellises, railings, fences and arbors. They can also grow over shrubs and up trees and can be used as groundcover.

Recommended

There are many species, hybrids and cultivars of clematis. The flower forms, blooming times and sizes of the plants can vary. Check with your local garden center to see what is available.

Jackman clematis (above), 'Gravetye Beauty' (below)

There are so many species, hybrids and cultivars of clematis that it is possible to have one in bloom all season.

Features: twining habit; early- to late-summer flowers; decorative seedheads
Flower color: blue, purple, pink, yellow, red, white **Height:** 10–17' (3–5 m) or more **Spread:** 5' (1.5 m) or more
Hardiness: zones 3–8

Climbing Hydrangea
Hydrangea

A mature climbing hydrangea can cover an entire wall, and with its dark, glossy leaves and delicate, lacy flowers, it is quite possibly one of the most stunning climbing plants available.

Growing
Hydrangeas prefer **partial or light shade** but tolerate both full sun and full shade. The soil should be of **average to high fertility, humus rich, moist** and **well drained**. These plants perform best in cool, moist conditions, so be sure to mulch their roots.

Tips
Climbing hydrangea climbs up trees, walls, fences, pergolas and arbors. It clings to walls by means of aerial roots, and therefore needs no support, just a somewhat textured surface, such as cinder or cement blocks. It also grows over rocks, can be used as a groundcover and can be trained to form a small tree or shrub.

Recommended
H. anomala subsp. *petiolaris* (*H. petiolaris*) is a clinging vine with dark, glossy green leaves that sometimes turn an attractive yellow in fall. For over a month in midsummer, the vine is covered with white, lacy-looking flowers, and the entire plant appears veiled in a lacy mist.

Features: flowers, clinging habit, exfoliating bark **Flower color:** white **Height:** 50–80' (15–25 m) **Spread:** 50–80' (15–25 m) **Hardiness:** zones 4–8

Cup-and-Saucer Vine

Cobaea

Cup-and-saucer vine, a vigorous climber native to Mexico, produces frilly, purple flowers from spring until frost.

Growing

Cup-and-saucer vine prefers **full sun**. The soil should be **well drained** and of **average fertility**. This plant is fond of hot weather and will do best if planted in a sheltered site with southern exposure. Set the seeds on edge when planting them, and barely cover them with soil.

Tips

Grow this vine up a trellis, over an arbor or along a chain-link fence. Cup-and-saucer vine requires a sturdy support to climb. It uses grabbing hooks to climb so it can't grow up a wall without something to grab. It can be trained to fill almost any space. In hanging baskets the vine will climb the hanger and spill over the edges.

Recommended

C. scandens is a vigorous climbing vine with flowers that are creamy green when they open and mature to deep purple. **Var. *alba*** has white flowers.

These tender plants can be cut back a bit in fall and overwintered indoors. Plants grown in hanging baskets are easiest to move indoors.

Also called: cathedral bells
Features: flowers, clinging habit, long blooming period **Flower color:** green changing to purple; white **Height:** 15–25' (4.5–7.5 m) **Spread:** 15–25' (4.5–7.5 m)
Hardiness: tender perennial treated as an annual

Grape
Vitis

Wine grape (above & below)

The grape's ripe fruit can attract wasps. You may wish to avoid planting this vine near the house if any family members are allergic to bee or wasp stings.

The grape vine's bold foliage and colorful fruit provide substance and a feel of permanence and weight that many new gardens need.

Growing
Grapes prefer **full sun** or **partial shade**. The soil should be **moist** and **acidic**. These plants tolerate most soil conditions as long as the soil is **well drained**.

Tips
Grape vines can be trained to grow on almost any sturdy structure. They may need to be tied in place until the basic structure is established.

Recommended
V. cognetiae (crimson glory vine) is a woody climber with attractive scarlet fall color. It bears inedible, small, dark purple fruit. (Zones 5–8)

V. rotundifolia (muscadine grape) bears purple or greenish purple fruit, which are edible but bitter. Fall color is yellow. (Zones 5–8)

V. vinifera (wine grape) is an attractive woody climber, best known for the wine grapes it produces. **'Purpurea'** is a good performer bearing deep purple foliage. (Zones 6–8)

Features: summer and fall foliage, late-summer to fall fruit **Habit:** woody, climbing, deciduous vine **Height:** 22–50' (7–15 m) **Spread:** 22–50' (7–15 m) **Hardiness:** zones 5–9

Hardy Kiwi

Actinidia

'Ananasnaya' hardy kiwi (above), hardy kiwi (below)

Hardy kiwi is handsome in its simplicity. Its lush green leaves, vigor and adaptability make it very useful, especially on difficult sites.

Growing

Hardy kiwi vines grow best in **full sun** and tolerate partial shade. The soil should be **fertile** and **well drained**. These plants require shelter from strong winds.

Tips

These vines need a sturdy structure to twine around. Pergolas, arbors and sufficiently large and sturdy fences provide good support. Given a trellis against a wall, a tree or some other upright structure, hardy kiwis will twine upward all summer. They can also be grown in containers.

Hardy kiwi vines can grow uncontrollably. Prune them back if they get out of hand.

Recommended

A. arguta (hardy kiwi, bower actinidia) has dark green, heart-shaped leaves, white flowers and smooth-skinned, greenish yellow, edible fruit.

A. kolomikta (variegated kiwi vine, kolomikta actinidia) has green leaves strongly variegated with white and pink, white flowers and smooth-skinned, greenish yellow, edible fruit.

Features: early-summer flowers, edible fruit, twining habit **Flower color:** white **Height:** 15–30' (4.5–9 m) to indefinite **Spread:** 15–30' (4.5–9 m) to indefinite **Hardiness:** zones 3–8

Honeysuckle
Lonicera

Honeysuckles can be rampant, twining vines, but with careful consideration and placement they won't overrun your garden. The fragrance of the flowers makes any effort worthwhile.

Growing
Honeysuckles grow well in **full sun** or **partial shade**. The soil should be **average to fertile, humus rich, moist** and **well drained**.

Tips
Honeysuckle can be trained to grow up a trellis, fence, arbor or other structure. In a large container near a porch it will ramble over the edges of the pot and up the railings with reckless abandon.

Recommended
Many cultivars and hybrids are available with flowers in yellow, red or scarlet, including *L.* x *brownii* 'Dropmore Scarlet,' one of the hardiest of the climbing honeysuckles, cold hardy to Zone 4. It bears bright red flowers for most of the summer.

L. caprifolium (Italian honeysuckle, Italian woodbine) bears fragrant, creamy white or yellow flowers in late spring and early summer.

L. sempervirens (trumpet honeysuckle, coral honeysuckle) bears orange or red flowers in late spring and early summer.

There are dozens of honeysuckle species, hybrids and cultivars. Check with your local garden center to see what is available.

'Dropmore Scarlet' (above & below)

Features: late-spring and early-summer flowers; twining habit; fruit **Flower color:** orange, red, yellow, creamy white **Height:** 6–20' (1.8–6 m) **Spread:** 6–20' (1.8–6 m) **Hardiness:** zones 5–8

Passion Flower
Passiflora

Passion flower is mesmerizing. Most are native to North America. Passion flower is actually a fast-growing woody climber that is grown as an annual. It can also be grown as a tender perennial west of the Cascade Mountains. It will thrive for years next to a house without any winter protection.

Growing

Grow passion flower in **full sun** or **partial shade**. This plant prefers **well-drained, moist** soil of **average fertility**. Keep it **sheltered** from wind and cold.

Tips

Passion flower is a popular addition to mixed containers and makes an unusual focal point near a door.

In spring, many garden centers sell small passion flower plants that quickly climb trellises and other supports over summer. They can be composted at the end of summer or cut back and brought inside to overwinter in a bright room.

The small, round fruits are edible but not very tasty.

Recommended

P. caerulea (blue passion flower) bears unusual, purple-banded, purple-white flowers all summer. **'Constance Elliott'** bears fragrant, white flowers.

Blue passion flower (above & below)

Fertilize passion flower sparingly. Too much nitrogen will encourage lots of foliage but few flowers.

Features: exotic flowers; habit; foliage
Flower color: white or pale pink petals with blue or purple bands **Height:** up to 30' (9 m)
Spread: variable **Hardiness:** zones 6–8

Sweet Pea

Lathyrus

Sweet peas are among the most enchanting annuals. Their fragrance is intoxicating.

Growing

Sweet peas prefer **full sun** but tolerate light shade. The soil should be **fertile, high in organic matter, moist** and **well drained**. The plants tolerate light frost. Fertilize very lightly during flowering season.

Soak seeds in water for 24 hours or nick them with a nail file before planting. Plant a second crop of sweet peas about a month after the first to ensure a longer blooming period.

Tips

Sweet peas will grow up poles, trellises and fences or over rocks. They cling by wrapping tendrils around whatever they are growing up, so they do best when they have a rough surface, chain-link fence, small twigs or a net to cling to.

Deadheading extends the blooming season. As soon as you allow blossoms to fade on this vine, it will stop flowering.

Recommended

There are many cultivars of **L. odoratus**, including some that are small and bushy rather than climbing. Heritage varieties are often the most fragrant.

Features: clinging habit, summer flowers
Flower color: pink, red, purple, lavender, blue, salmon, pale yellow, peach, white or bicolored **Height:** 12"–6' (30 cm–1.8 m)
Spread: 6–12" (15–30 cm)
Hardiness: hardy annual

Virginia Creeper
Parthenocissus

Virginia creeper (above & below)

*L*et a Virginia creeper adorn any garden that needs a look of wild abandon. Virginia creeper lights a wildfire of color each fall.

Growing
These vines grow well in any light from **full sun to full shade**. The soil should be **fertile** and **well drained**. The plants will adapt to clay or sandy soils.

Tips
Virginia creepers do not require support because they have clinging rootlets that adhere to just about any surface, even smooth wood, vinyl or metal. Give the plants lots of space and let them cover a wall, fence or arbor. They can also be used as groundcovers.

Recommended
These two species are very similar, except for the shape of the leaves. The **fruits** are **poisonous.**

P. quinquefolia (Virginia creeper, woodbine) has dark green foliage. Each leaf, divided into five leaflets, turns flaming red in fall.

P. tricuspidata (Boston ivy, Japanese creeper) has dark green, three-lobed leaves that turn red in fall. This species is not quite as hardy as *P. quinquefolia*.

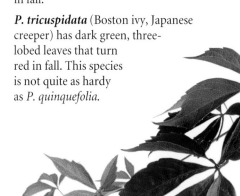

Also called: Boston ivy **Features:** summer and fall foliage, clinging habit **Height:** 30–70' (9–21 m) **Spread:** 30–70' (9–21 m) **Hardiness:** zones 3–8

Wisteria
Wisteria

Chinese wisteria (above & below)

Loose clusters of purple hang like lace from the branches of wisteria. With prudent pruning, a gardener can create beautiful tree forms and arbor specimens.

Growing

Wisterias grow well in **full sun** or **partial shade**. The soil should be of **average fertility, moist** and **well drained**. Too fertile a soil will produce lots of vegetative growth but very few flowers. Avoid planting wisteria near a lawn where fertilizer may leach over to your vine.

Tips

These vines require something to twine around, such as an arbor or other sturdy structure. Select a permanent site; wisterias don't like being moved. They may send up suckers, and can root wherever branches touch the ground. All parts of these plants are **poisonous**.

Recommended

W. floribunda (Japanese wisteria) bears long, pendulous clusters of fragrant blue, purple, pink or white flowers in late spring before the leaves emerge. Long, bean-like pods follow.

W. sinensis (Chinese wisteria) bears long, pendant clusters of fragrant, blue-purple flowers in late spring. **'Alba'** has white flowers.

To keep wisteria blooming sporadically all summer, prune off flowering spikes as soon as the flowers fade. A long-handled pole pruner works well. Wisteria will send out new blooming shoots until frost.

Features: late-spring flowers, foliage, twining habit **Flower color:** blue, purple, pink, white **Height:** 20–50' (6–15 m) or more **Spread:** 20–50' (6–15 m) or more **Hardiness:** zones 4–8

Asiatic Lily
Lilium

Lilies in mixed planting (above), 'Stargazer' (below)

*A*siatic lily produces decorative clusters of large, richly colored blooms at different times of the season depending on the hybrid. If you plant a variety of cultivars, you can have lilies blooming all season.

Growing

Lilies grow best in **full sun**, but they like to have their **roots shaded**. The soil should be **rich in organic matter, fertile, moist** and **well drained**.

Tips

Lilies are often grouped in beds and borders and can be naturalized in woodland gardens and near water features. They look great in the back of the bed or in the center of a flower display. These plants are narrow but tall; plant at least three plants together to create some volume.

Recommended

The many species, hybrids and cultivars available are grouped by type. Check with your local garden center for what's available locally. **Asiatic hybrids** bear clusters of flowers in early or mid-summer and are available in a wide range of colors. **Oriental hybrids** bear clusters of large, fragrant flowers in mid- and late summer. Colors are usually white, pink or red.

Lily bulbs should be planted in fall before the first frost, but can also be planted in spring if bulbs are available.

Also called: Oriental lily **Features:** early-, mid- or late-season flowers in various colors **Flower color:** orange, yellow, peach, pink, purple, red, white **Height:** 24"–5' (60 cm–1.5 m) **Spread:** 12" (30 cm) **Hardiness:** zones 4–8

Crocosmia

Crocosmia

'Lucifer' (above), 'Norwich Canary' (below)

The intense colors of crocosmias are like beacons in the garden.

Growing

Crocosmias prefer **full sun**. The soil should be of **average fertility, humus rich, moist** and **well drained**. Plant in a protected area and mulch in fall with shredded leaves or other organic matter to protect the roots from fluctuating winter temperatures. Near the coast and in well-drained soil, crocosmia will overwinter without additional winter protection. Overgrown clumps produce few flowers.

Tips

Crocosmias look striking when massed in a herbaceous or mixed border. They look good next to a pond, where the brightly colored flowers can be reflected in the water.

Recommended

C. x *crocosmiflora* is a spreading plant with long, strap-like leaves and one-sided spikes of red, orange or yellow mid- and late-summer flowers. **'Citronella'** (golden fleece) bears bright yellow flowers.

C. **'Lucifer,'** the hardiest of the bunch, bears bright, scarlet red flowers. Hummingbirds will love you for planting it.

In cold winter areas, crocosmia corms can be dug up in fall and stored in slightly damp sawdust or peat moss in a cool, dark place. Monitor them regularly. When they sprout, pot them and move them to a well-lit but cool room until planting out after the risk of frost has passed.

Features: brightly colored flowers, strap-like foliage
Flower color: shades of red, orange and yellow
Height: 18"–4' (45 cm–1.2 m) **Spread:** 12–18"
(30–45 cm) **Hardiness:** zones 5–8

Crocus
Crocus

Crocuses are harbingers of spring. Their bright, cheerful colors will melt away your winter blahs. They often appear in full bloom, as if by magic, from beneath melting snow.

Growing

Crocuses grow well in **full sun** or **light, dappled shade**. The soil should be of **poor to average fertility**, **gritty** and **well drained**. Plant corms about 4" (10 cm) deep in fall.

Tips

Crocuses are almost always planted in groups. Drifts of crocuses planted in lawns provide early color while the grass remains dormant. In beds and borders they can be left to naturalize. Plants will fill in and spread out to provide a bright welcome in spring.

Try planting crocuses under deciduous trees and shrubs. They look great under the skirt of a weeping Japanese maple or as an accent for forsythia.

Recommended

Many crocus species, hybrids and cultivars are available. The familiar spring-flowering crocus is *C.* **x** *vernus* (Dutch crocus). Cultivars are available with flowers in shades of purple, yellow and white, sometimes bicolored or with darker veins.

Features: early-spring flowers **Flower color:** purple, yellow, white and bicolored **Height:** 2–6" (5–15 cm) **Spread:** 2–4" (5–10 cm) **Hardiness:** zones 3–8

Daffodil

Narcissus

Many gardeners automatically think of large, yellow, trumpet-shaped flowers when they think of daffodils, but there is a wide range of color, form and size among the many varieties.

Growing

Daffodils grow best in **full sun** or **light, dappled shade**. The soil should be **average to fertile, moist** and **well drained**. Bulbs should be planted in fall. The bigger the bulb the deeper it should be planted. A rule of thumb is to measure the bulb from top to bottom and multiply that number by three to know how deep to plant.

Tips

Plant daffodils where they can be left to naturalize—in the light shade beneath a tree or in a woodland garden. In mixed beds and borders, the faded leaves are hidden by the summer foliage of other plants. Large-leaved perennials such as hosta and lady's mantle make fine companion plants.

Recommended

Many species, hybrids and cultivars of daffodils are available. Flowers may be borne solitary or in clusters. There are 12 different flower form categories.

The cup in the center of a daffodil is called the corona, and the group of petals and sepals that surrounds the corona is called the perianth.

Features: spring flowers **Flower color:** white, yellow, peach, orange, pink and bicolored **Height:** 4–24" (10–60 cm) **Spread:** 4–12" (10–30 cm) **Hardiness:** zones 3–8

Dahlia

Dahlia

*T*he variation in size, shape and color of dahlia flowers is astonishing. You are sure to find at least one that appeals to you.

Growing

Dahlias prefer **full sun** and **fertile, moist, well-drained soil** rich in **organic matter**. Deadhead to keep plants tidy and blooming.

Tubers can be purchased and started early indoors. Tubers can also be dug up in fall and stored in slightly moist peat moss. Pot them up and place them in a bright room when they start sprouting in mid- to late winter.

Tips

Dahlias make attractive, colorful additions to a mixed border. Smaller varieties are good edging plants and larger ones make good alternatives to shrubs. Attractive varieties with interesting and unusual flowers are also available.

Recommended

Of the many dahlia hybrids, most are grown from tubers but a few can be started from seed. Several hybrids are sold based on flower shape. The flowers are 2–12" (5–30 cm) across and are available in various colors.

To overwinter tubers near the coast, cut the stems back after the first frost and mulch heavily. Use a tarp or waterproof cover to keep tubers from rotting during our wet winters.

Features: summer flowers, attractive foliage, bushy habit **Flower color:** purple, pink, white, yellow, orange, red and bicolored **Height:** 8"–5' (20 cm–1.5 m) **Spread:** 8–18" (20–45 cm) **Hardiness:** tender perennials grown as annuals

Flowering Onion
Allium

Giant onion (above), nodding onion (below)

Flowering onions, with their striking, ball-like or loose, nodding clusters of flowers, are sure to attract attention.

Growing

Flowering onions grow best in **full sun**. The soil should be **average to fertile, moist** and **well drained**. Plant bulbs in fall.

Tips

Flowering onions work best in groups in a bed or border where they can be left to naturalize. Most will self-seed when left to their own devices. The foliage, which tends to fade just as the plants come into flower,

can be hidden with groundcover or a low, bushy companion plant.

After flowering onions bloom, leave their flowerheads to dry on the stems. The dry flowers provide a starry feature all summer.

Recommended

Several flowering onion species, hybrids and cultivars have gained popularity for their decorative flowers. *A. aflatunense* has dense, globe-like clusters of lavender flowers. *A. caeruleum* (blue globe onion) bears globe-like clusters of blue flowers. *A. cernuum* (nodding onion, wild onion) has loose, drooping clusters of pink flowers. *A. giganteum* (giant onion) is a towering plant with large, globe-shaped clusters of pinky purple flowers.

Features: summer flowers, cylindrical or strap-shaped leaves Flower color: pink, purple, white, yellow, blue, maroon Height: 6"–6$^{1}/_{2}$' (15 cm–2 m) Spread: 2–12" (5–30 cm) Hardiness: zones 3–8

Snowdrop
Galanthus

*W*hen winter has you feeling dull and dreary, let early-blooming snowdrops bring some much-needed color to your winter garden.

Growing

Snowdrops grow well in **full sun to partial shade** in **fertile, well-drained, moist, humus-rich** soil. Do not allow the soil to dry out in summer.

Tips

Snowdrops work well in beds, borders and rock gardens. They should always be planted in groups and close to each other for the best effect. Snowdrops can be planted in the lawn or under deciduous shrubs and trees that will provide part shade in the summer. These plants are great for naturalizing in lightly shaded woodlands.

Recommended

G. elwesii (giant snowdrop) has larger flowers and foliage, and grows taller than *G. nivalis*. The inner petals are heavily marked with green.

G. nivalis (common snowdrop) is a tiny plant that produces small, nodding, honey-scented, white flowers in mid- to late winter. The inner petals are marked with a green 'V' shape. Cultivars are available, some with double flowers and some with yellow markings instead of green.

The various snowdrop species hybridize easily with each other; many hybrids are available.

Giant snowdrop with winter aconite (above), common snowdrop (below)

All parts of snowdrop are poisonous if ingested. Handling the bulbs may irritate sensitive skin.

Features: early-blooming flowers, strap-like foliage, easy to grow **Flower color:** white **Height:** 4–12" (10–30 cm) **Spread:** 4–6" (10–15 cm) **Hardiness:** zones 3–8

Tulip

Tulipa

Tulips with basket-of-gold (above)

Tulips, with their beautifully colored flowers, are a welcome sight in the first warm days of spring.

Growing

Tulips grow best in **full sun**. The flowers tend to bend toward the light in partial or light shade. The soil should be **fertile** and **well drained**. Plant bulbs in fall. Cold-treated bulbs can be planted in spring. Though tulips can repeat bloom, many hybrids perform best if planted new each year. Species and older cultivars are the best choice for naturalizing.

When choosing tulip bulbs, remember that the bigger the bulb, the bigger the bloom.

Tips

Tulips provide the best display when mass planted in flowerbeds and borders. They can also be grown in containers and forced to bloom early in indoor pots. Some species and older cultivars can be naturalized in meadow and wildflower gardens.

Recommended

There are about 100 species of tulips and thousands of hybrids and cultivars. They are generally divided into 15 groups based on bloom time and flower appearance. They come in dozens of shades, with many bicolored and multi-colored varieties. Blue is the only color not available. Purchase your tulips in early fall for the best selection.

Features: spring flowers **Flower color:** all colors except blue **Height:** 6–30" (15–75 cm) **Spread:** 2–8" (5–20 cm) **Hardiness:** zones 3–8; often grown as annuals

Basil

Ocimum

The sweet, fragrant leaves of fresh basil add a delicious flavor to salads and tomato-based dishes.

Growing

Basil grows best in a **warm, sheltered** location in **full sun**. The soil should be **fertile, moist** and **well drained**. Pinch tips regularly to encourage bushy growth. Plant out or direct-sow seed after frost danger has passed in spring.

Tips

Though basil will grow best in a warm spot outdoors in the garden, it can be grown successfully in an indoor pot by a bright window to provide you with fresh leaves all year.

Recommended

O. basilicum is one of the most popular of the culinary herbs. There are dozens of varieties including ones with large or tiny, green or purple and smooth or ruffled leaves. Cultivars of varying height are also available.

'Genovese' & 'Cinnamon' (above), 'Genovese' (below)

Basil is a good companion plant for tomatoes—both like warm, moist growing conditions and when you pick tomatoes for a salad you'll also remember to include a few sprigs or leaves of basil.

Features: fragrant, decorative leaves
Height: 6–24" (15–60 cm) **Spread:** 6–18"
(15–45 cm) **Hardiness:** tender annual

Chives
Allium

The delicate onion flavor of chives is best enjoyed fresh. Mix chives into dips or sprinkle them on salads and baked potatoes.

Growing

Chives grow best in **full sun**. The soil should be **fertile, moist** and **well drained**, but chives adapt to most soil conditions. These plants are easy to start from seed, but the soil temperature must be consistently above 66° F (19° C) before they will germinate, so seeds started directly in the garden are unlikely to sprout before early summer.

Tips

Chives are decorative enough to be included in a mixed or herbaceous border and can be left to naturalize. In a herb garden, chives should be given plenty of space to allow self-seeding.

Recommended

A. schoenoprasum forms a clump of bright green, cylindrical leaves. Clusters of pinky purple flowers are produced in early and mid-summer. Varieties with white or pink flowers are available.

Features: foliage, form, flowers
Flower color: pink, purple, white **Height:** 8–24" (20–60 cm) **Spread:** 12" (30 cm) or more
Hardiness: zones 3–8

Coriander•Cilantro
Coriandrum

Coriander is a multi-purpose herb. The leaves, called cilantro, are used in salads, salsas and soups. The seeds, called coriander, are used in pies, chutneys and marmalades. Each has a distinct flavor and different culinary uses.

Growing

Coriander prefers **full sun**, but tolerates partial shade. The soil should be **fertile, light** and **well drained**. These plants dislike humid conditions and do best during a dry summer.

Tips

Coriander has pungent leaves and is best planted where people will not have to brush past it. It is, however, a delight to behold when in flower. Add a plant or two throughout your borders and vegetable garden, both for the visual appeal and to attract beneficial insects.

Recommended

C. sativum forms a clump of lacy basal foliage above which large, loose clusters of tiny, white flowers are produced. The seeds ripen in late summer and fall.

basal leaves (above), upper leaves (below)

The delicate, cloud-like clusters of flowers attract pollinating insects such as butterflies and bees as well as abundant predatory insects that will help keep pest insects to a minimum.

Features: form, foliage, flowers, seeds
Flower color: white **Height:** 16–24" (40–60 cm)
Spread: 8–16" (20–40 cm)
Hardiness: tender annual

Lavender

Lavandula

English lavender (above & below)

Lavender has antibacterial and anti-fungal properties and a sharp, clean scent. Its essential oil can relax yet energize the nervous system.

Growing

Lavenders grow best in **full sun** in **very well-drained, alkaline, average to fertile** soil. Established plants are heat and drought tolerant. *L. x intermedia* can be sensitive to winter cold and should be planted out of winter winds.

In colder areas, cover lavenders with mulch and a good layer of snow. Good drainage is essential to winter survival—often, winterkill results from wet feet, not from cold.

Tips

Lavenders are deer-resistant, and can be used as edging plants and in low hedges. Plant with other drought-tolerant specimens, such as pinks and thyme.

Recommended

L. angustifolia (English lavender) is an aromatic, bushy sub-shrub that is often treated as a perennial. It bears spikes of small flowers in shades of violet-blue. Cultivars come in different sizes, with flowers in shades of purple, blue and pink.

L. x intermedia (lavandin) is a hybrid of English lavender and spike lavender (*L. latifolia*). The flowers are held on long spikes.

Features: fragrance, summer to fall flowers, foliage **Flower color:** shades of purple, blue and pink **Height:** 8–36" (20–90 cm) **Spread:** up to 4' (1.2 m) **Hardiness:** zones 5–9

Mint

Mentha

The cool, refreshing flavor of mint lends itself to tea and other hot or cold beverages. Mint sauce, made from freshly chopped leaves, is often served with lamb.

Growing

Mint grows well in **full sun** and **partial shade**. The soil should be **average to fertile, humus rich** and **moist**. Mint spreads vigorously by rhizomes and may need a barrier in the soil to restrict its spread.

Tips

Mint is a good groundcover for damp spots. Try planting it under a hose bib where the dripping water will encourage thick growth that blocks out weeds. It grows well along ditches that may only be periodically wet. It also can be used in beds and borders, but may overwhelm less vigorous plants.

The flowers attract bees, butterflies and other pollinators to the garden.

Recommended

There are many species, hybrids and cultivars of mint. **M. spicata** (spearmint), **M. x piperita** (peppermint) and **M. x piperita citrata** (orange mint) are three of the most commonly grown culinary varieties. More decorative varieties with variegated or curly leaves as well as varieties with unusual, fruit-scented leaves are also available.

M. x gracilis 'Variegata' (variegated ginger mint) has attractive, bright green and gold, variegated foliage that has a strong, fruity mint aroma and ginger flavor.

Peppermint with lemon balm (above), variegated ginger mint (below)

A few sprigs of fresh mint in a pitcher of iced tea gives it an added zip.

Features: fragrant foliage, summer flowers
Flower color: purple, pink or white
Height: 6–36" (15–90 cm) **Spread:** 36" (90 cm) or more **Hardiness:** zones 4–8

Oregano·Marjoram
Origanum

'Polyphant' oregano (above), 'Aureum' oregano (below)

In Greek, oros means 'mountain' and ganos means 'joy,' so oregano translates as 'joy of the mountain.'

Oregano and marjoram are two of the best known and most frequently used herbs. They are popular in stuffings, soups and stews, and no pizza is complete until it's sprinkled with fresh or dried oregano leaves.

Growing
Oregano and marjoram grow best in **full sun**. The soil should be of **poor to average fertility, neutral to alkaline** and **well drained**. The flowers attract pollinators to the garden.

Tips
These bushy perennials make a lovely addition to any border and can be trimmed to form low hedges. Low-growing oregano does well in the rock garden and looks especially attractive combined with variegated and golden sage.

Recommended
O. majorana (marjoram) is an upright plant with light green, hairy leaves. It produces white or pink flowers in summer and can be grown as an annual where it is not hardy.

O. vulgare hirtum (oregano, Greek oregano) is the most flavorful culinary variety. It is low-growing and has hairy, gray-green leaves and white flowers. Many interesting varieties are available with golden, variegated or curly leaves.

Features: fragrant foliage, summer flowers, bushy habit
Flower color: white or pink **Height:** 12–32" (30–80 cm)
Spread: 8–18" (20–45 cm) **Hardiness:** zones 5–8

Parsley
Petroselinum

Parsley in a mixed planter (above)

Though usually used as a garnish, parsley is rich in vitamins and minerals and is reputed to freshen the breath after garlic or onion-rich foods are eaten.

Growing
Parsley grows well in **full sun** or **partial shade**. The soil should be of **average to rich fertility, humus rich, moist** and **well drained**.

Parsley resents transplanting and should be started where you mean to grow it. Direct sow seeds into warm soil or keep the soil warm with a frost sleeve, cloche, row cover or portable cold frame. If you start seeds early, use peat pots or pellets to avoid root disturbance.

Tips
Containers of parsley can be kept close to the house for easy picking. The bright foliage and compact growth habit make parsley a good edging plant for beds and borders.

Recommended
P. crispum forms a clump of bright green, divided leaves. This plant is a biennial usually grown as an annual. Cultivars may have flat or curly leaves. Flat leaves are more flavorful and curly leaves are more decorative. Dwarf cultivars are available.

Features: attractive foliage **Height:** 8–24"
(20–60 cm) **Spread:** 12–24" (30–60 cm)
Hardiness: zones 5–8; often grown as an annual

Rosemary
Rosmarinus

Rosemary's needle-like leaves are used to flavor a wide variety of culinary dishes, including chicken, pork, lamb, rice, tomato and egg dishes.

Growing
Rosemary prefers **full sun**, but tolerates partial shade. The soil should be of **poor to average fertility** and **well drained**.

Grow rosemary in shrub borders where it's hardy, or plant it in a container as a specimen. Low-growing, spreading plants can be included in rock gardens, along the top of retaining walls or in hanging baskets.

Tips
To overwinter a container-grown plant, keep it in very light or partial shade in summer, then transfer it to a sunny window indoors for winter. Keep it well watered, but not soaking wet.

Removing the woody branches encourages fresh new growth.

Recommended
R. officinalis is a dense, bushy, evergreen shrub with narrow, dark green leaves. Cultivar habits vary from strongly upright to prostrate and spreading. Flowers usually come in shades of blue, but pink-flowered cultivars are available. Some cultivars can survive in zone 6 in a sheltered location with winter protection. Plants rarely reach their mature size when grown in containers.

Cut woody spears of rosemary and use for spearing meat chunks for the barbecue.

Features: fragrant, evergreen foliage; summer flowers **Flower color:** bright blue, sometimes pink **Height:** 8"–4' (20 cm–1.2 m) **Spread:** 12"–4' (30 cm–1.2 m) **Hardiness:** zone 8

Sage
Salvia

Sage is perhaps the best-known flavoring for stuffing, but it has a great range of uses, including in soups, stews, sausages and dumplings.

Growing
Sage prefers **full sun** but tolerates light shade. The soil should be of **average fertility** and **well drained**. These plants benefit from light mulching with compost each year. They are drought tolerant once established.

Tips
Sage is an attractive plant for the border; it adds volume to the middle of the border and makes an attractive edging or feature plant near the front. Sage can also be grown in mixed planters and is a long-lived standard in rock gardens.

Recommended
S. officinalis is a woody, mounding plant with soft, gray-green leaves. Spikes of light purple flowers appear in early and mid-summer. Many cultivars with attractive foliage are available, including the silver-leaved **'Berggarten,'** the yellow-margined **'Icterina,'** the purple-leaved **'Purpurea'** and the cream variegated **'Tricolor,'** which has a pink flush to the new growth.

'Icternia' (above), 'Purpurea' (below)

Sage has been used since at least ancient Greek times as a medicinal and culinary herb and continues to be widely used for both those purposes today.

Features: fragrant, decorative foliage; summer flowers   **Flower color:** blue or purple   **Height:** 12–24" (30–60 cm)   **Spread:** 18–36" (45–90 cm)   **Hardiness:** zones 5–8

Thyme
Thymus

Carpet of wooly thyme (above), lemon-scented thyme (below)

Once plants finish flowering, shear them back by about one-half to encourage new growth and prevent the plants from becoming too woody.

Thyme is a popular culinary herb used in soups, stews and casseroles, and with roasts.

Growing
Thyme prefers **full sun**. The soil should be **neutral to alkaline** and of **poor to average fertility. Very good drainage** is essential. It is beneficial to work some leaf mold into the soil.

Tips
Thyme works well in sunny, dry locations at the front of borders, between or beside paving stones, on rock gardens and rock walls, and in containers. Creeping thyme makes a good lawn substitute.

Recommended
*T. x **citriodorus*** (lemon-scented thyme) forms a mound of lemon-scented, dark green foliage with pale pink flowers. Cultivars with silver- or gold-margined leaves are available.

T. praecox subsp. *arcticus* (*T. serpyllum*, mother of thyme, creeping thyme, wild thyme) is a low-growing variety with purple flowers. Many cultivars are available. **'Elfin'** forms tiny, dense mounds of foliage. **'Lanuginosis'** (woolly thyme) is mat forming with fuzzy, gray-green leaves and pink or purple flowers.

T. vulgaris (common thyme) forms a bushy mound of dark green leaves and purple, pink or white flowers. Cultivars with variegated leaves are available.

Features: bushy habit; fragrant, decorative foliage; flowers **Flower color:** purple, pink or white **Height:** 2–16" (5–40 cm) **Spread:** 4–16" (10–40 cm) **Hardiness:** zones 4–8

Black Mondo Grass
Ophiopogon

Black mondo grass is an excellent accent and contrast plant. A black background highlights any brightly colored plants or flowers.

Growing

Black mondo grass prefers to grow in **full sun to light shade** in **moist, moderately fertile, well-drained, humus-rich** soil. The foliage is at its best in full sun. Divide in spring just as new growth resumes. These plants appreciate some winter protection of thick mulch in zones 5 and 6.

Tips

Because it spreads by rhizomes, black mondo grass can be used as a dense groundcover and for erosion control. Use it for border edges and containers. It can be used as a bedding plant in cooler zones, and can be dug up and stored for winter in a cool, dark room.

Recomended

O. planiscapus **'Ebknizam'** (EBONY NIGHT) has curving, almost black leaves and dark lavender flowers. It grows 4–6" (10–15 cm) tall and 6–12" (15–30 cm) wide. **'Nigrescens'** has curving, almost black foliage and pink to white-flushed pink flowers. It grows 6–12" (15–30 cm) tall and 12" (30 cm) wide. Both cultivars produce blackish, berry-like fruit.

'Nigrescens' (above), 'Ebknizam' (below)

This plant is a member of the same family as lilies, and does not like being mowed.

Also called: black lilyturf **Features:** uniquely colored foliage **Flower color:** lavender, pink, white-flushed pink **Height:** 4–12" (10–30 cm)
Spread: 6–12" (15–30 cm)
Hardiness: zones 5–9

Blue Fescue
Festuca

'Elijah Blue' (above), blue fescue (below)

Blue fescue was one of the first ornamental grasses to appear on the market over a decade ago. Blue fescue continues to display its finest features in harsh conditions.

Growing
Fescue prefers **full sun** in **poor to moderately fertile, well-drained** soil. Keep the soil a little on the **dry** side.

Tips
The low-growing tufts of blue fescue are used as edging for beds and borders, and look great mass planted. It is frequently used in xeriscape settings and naturalized areas. The low-growing fescues also work well in rock and alpine gardens.

Recommended
F. glauca (*F. ovina* var. *glauca*; blue fescue, blue sheep's fescue) produces steely blue tufts of fine, needle-like blades of grass. Most varieties produce tan-colored flower spikes that rise above the mounds of blue foliage. A great many cultivars and hybrids are available. **'Elijah Blue'** has soft, powdery blue foliage.

Features: colorful foliage, flower spikes, growth habit **Height:** 6–18" (15–45 cm) **Spread:** 10–12" (25–30 cm) **Hardiness:** zones 3–8

Golden Hakone Grass

Hakonechloa

Golden Hakone grass is one of the most beautiful ornamental grasses available today. The striking foliage cascades nicely over the edges of containers or low borders.

Growing

Golden Hakone grass grows well in **partial to light shade** in **moist, well-drained, moderately fertile, humus-rich** soil. The leaf color is enhanced in partial to light shade. Golden Hakone can tolerate full shade but its foliage will turn lime green under such conditions. It also tolerates full sun as long as the soil remains moist. Divide in spring. Avoid locations with cold, drying winds.

Tips

Golden Hakone grass works well at the edge of a woodland garden, but is also very effective in containers, beds, borders and rock gardens. It makes an excellent addition to larger gardens where it can be planted in drifts.

Recomended

H. macra **'Aureola'** is a slow-spreading, mound-forming, perennial grass with lush, cascading foliage. It has yellow foliage with narrow green stripes. The foliage adopts a bronze to pinkish red tint in fall before it dies back in winter. The variegated cultivars are more popular than the species.

This slow-growing grass is very well behaved and will not invade its neighbors.

Also called: Japanese forest grass **Features:** colorful, decorative, strap-like foliage; fall color
Height: 10–18" (25–45 cm) **Spread:** $2^{1}/_{2}$–3' (75–90 cm) **Hardiness:** zones 5–9

Japanese Painted Fern
Athyrium

'Pictum' (above & below)

Japanese painted ferns are striking plants that add wonderful color to an otherwise shady green landscape.

Growing
Japanese painted fern requires **partial shade** in order to maintain its colorful foliage. If it is planted in full shade, the color may not develop, whereas full sun will cause the color to fade or the leaves to scorch. The soil should be **moderately fertile, moist, neutral to acidic** and **humus rich**. Divide in spring when necessary.

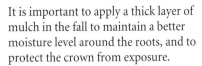

It is important to apply a thick layer of mulch in the fall to maintain a better moisture level around the roots, and to protect the crown from exposure.

Tips
Japanese painted fern looks very attractive planted en masse in mixed borders or shade gardens. The interesting foliage stands out among other ferns in a woodland setting.

Recommended
A. nipponicum is a creeping, compact fern that bears long, mid-green fronds with reddish purple midribs. The cultivars are far more readily available and attractive than the species. They come in a variety of foliage colors, with new additions yearly.

Features: attractive foliage **Flower color:** grown for foliage **Height:** 12–24" (30–60 cm) **Spread:** 12–24" (30–60 cm) **Hardiness:** zones 4–8

Japanese Silver Grass

Miscanthus

One of the most widely grown ornamental grasses available, Japanese silver grass offers vivid colors and ornamental plumes, and needs little maintenance. There is a vast array of species and cultivars to choose from, and most are hardy across our region.

Growing

Japanese silver grass prefers to grow in **full sun** in **moderately moist**, **fertile**, **well-drained** soil, but it will tolerate a variety of conditions.

Tips

Japanese silver grass is most effective when massed in a naturalized area or mixed border. Some varieties can grow quite large and are best displayed as specimens. If left alone in fall and winter, the dried foliage and showy plumes look very attractive, especially in areas that receive snow.

Recommended

M. sinsesis is a perennial, clumping grass. Its many cultivars and hybrids available offer variegated, striped or speckled foliage of one or more colors and tall, ornate, persistent plumes. **'Morning Light'** grows 4–5' (1.2–1.5 m) tall and 3–4' (90 cm–1.2 m) wide and bears green foliage edged with white and reddish bronze flowers.

'Purpurascens' (above), 'Zebrinus' (below)

Also called: Chinese silver grass, Eulalia grass, maiden grass **Features:** colorful, decorative, strap-like foliage and showy plumes; winter interest **Height:** 3–8' (90 cm–2.4 m) **Spread:** 2–4' (60 cm–1.2 m) **Hardiness:** zones 3–8

Maidenhair Fern

Adiantium

Maidenhair fern is often found growing in shady, moist locations beside streams or creeks. It is a non-invasive plant that spreads slowly and looks good planted with other shade-loving plants such as astilbe, fringed bleeding heart, hosta, lungwort and toad lily.

Growing

Maidenhair fern prefers **partial to full shade** and **moist, well-drained, fertile** soil.

Adiantium species have been used to cure bronchitis, coughs and asthma. They are also known as good hair tonics and restoratives.

Tips

Maidenhair fern works best at the edge of a woodland garden. It makes a good addition to a shaded border or a shaded rock garden. Maidenhair fern also does well in a streamside planting.

This fern is easy to propagate in the fall. Just slice off a section of the thick root mass and replant in a cool spot.

Recommended

A. pedatum (northern maidenhair fern) is a deciduous, upright plant that bears branched, horizontally oriented, lance-shaped fronds and lobed, fan-shaped, mid-green foliage that turns yellow-green to yellow in the fall. The leaflets have a waxy coating that rapidly sheds water and raindrops. The stems are dark brown to black.

Features: attractive foliage **Flower color:** plant grown for foliage **Height:** 12–24" (30–60 cm) **Spread:** 12–24" (30–60 cm) **Hardiness:** zones 3–8

Ostrich Fern

Matteuccia

These easy-to-grow ferns are appreciated as much for their delicious, emerging spring fronds as for their ornamental foliage and habit.

Growing

Ostrich fern prefers **partial or light shade**, but tolerates full shade. It can take full sun in cooler climates provided the soil remains moist. Soil should be **average to fertile, humus rich, neutral to acidic** and **moist**. Divide in spring.

Tips

This fern appreciates a moist woodland garden and is often found growing wild along the edges of woodland streams and creeks. Useful in shaded borders, these plants are quick to spread, to the delight of those who have tasted the delicate young fronds.

Recommended

M. struthiopteris (*M. pennsylvanica*) forms a circular cluster of slightly arching fronds. Stiff, brown, fertile fronds poke up in the center of the cluster in late summer and persist through winter.

Fresh fiddleheads are available at grocery stores in spring. Or buy them frozen all year.

Also called: fiddlehead fern **Features:** foliage, habit **Height:** 3–5' (90 cm–1.5 m) **Spread:** 12–36" (30–90 cm) or more **Hardiness:** zones 2–8

Phormium

Phormium

P. tenax 'Purpureum' (above), *P. tenax* cultivar (below)

These bold and impressive plants create quite an impact. They will become the focal point of any planting.

Growing

Phormium grows best in **full sun** in **fertile, moist, well-drained** soil. Plants grown in containers can be overwintered in a bright, cool, frost-free location. Many phormiums survive the winters for years near the coast. *P. cookianum* and *P.* hybrids (*P. cookianum* x *P. tenax*) appreciate shade from the hot afternoon sun.

Tips

Use phormium in beds, borders and container plantings. It looks good near entryways and walkways.

Recommended

There is a wide selection of available species, hybrids and cultivars. These plants have broad, strap-shaped leaves that come in a wide variety of colors. Many plants mature at over 6' (1.8 m) tall, with equal spreads, but when grown as annuals they rarely get this big. Dwarf cultivars that grow to about 24" (60 cm) are also available. Plants with bronze foliage are the hardiest selections.

Also called: New Zealand flax **Features:** colorful green, black, red or yellow, often multicolored and striped foliage **Height:** 2–8' (60 cm–2.2 m) **Spread:** 2–8' (60 cm–2.2 m) **Hardiness:** zones 8–10

Purple Fountain Grass

Pennisetum

Purple fountain grass makes a striking impact, especially when it anchors a container planting.

Growing

Purple fountain grass grows best in **full sun,** in **light, well-drained, moderately fertile** soil.

Tips

This ornamental grass can be planted in beds and borders, en masse, as a specimen or accent plant, and in a rock garden.

Purple fountain grass can be dug up, brought inside and stored in a cool room for winter. If it has been grown in a container, cut back the foliage in fall and store the whole container. Make sure the root mass remains moist. This plant's seeds are sterile, and it must be propagated vegetatively.

Recommended

P. setaceum **'Rubrum'** ('Purpureum') is a dense, mound-forming, tender perennial grass that grows 3–5' (90 cm–1.5 m) tall and 18–36" (45–90 cm) wide. It has narrow, dark purple foliage and large, showy, rose red flower spikes from mid-summer to fall. **'Burgundy Giant'** can grow 6' (1.8 m) tall and 2–4' (60 cm–1.2 m) wide, and has wide, deep burgundy purple foliage. Its nodding flower spikes are pinkish purple and up to 15" (38 cm) long. It is hardy to zone 10.

'Rubrum' (above & below)

The foliage of purple fountain grass turns brown and dry in winter and can be a fire hazard.

Features: colorful foliage; large, fuzzy flower spikes; graceful habit **Height:** 2–6' (60 cm–1.8 m) **Spread:** 18"–4' (45 cm–1.2 m) **Hardiness:** zones 9–10; also grown as an annual

Reed Grass
Calamagrostis

'Karl Foerster' (above & below)

Reed grass is one of the first ornamental grasses to grow and bloom. It is highly sought after and frequently used by landscape designers who appreciate its upright form and early growth.

Growing

Reed grass thrives in **full to partial sun** in **moist, humus-rich, well-drained** soil. It is tolerant of dry soils, wet soils, clay soils, heat and drought. Divide in spring.

Tips

Reed grass works best as a vertical accent plant in beds, borders and containers.

Cut the plant back to about 3–4" above the ground in late winter to early spring before the new growth begins.

Recommended

C. x *acutiflora* is a slow-growing, upright perennial grass with arching, narrow, green foliage and tall, wiry stems that bear silvery bronze to pinkish purple panicles of flowers. Decorative cultivars are available in varied sizes and colors. **'Karl Foerster'** was the Perennial Plant Associations 2001 Plant of the Year.

Also called: smallweed, feather reed grass
Features: decorative flower stems, foliage, habit
Height: 2–6' (60–1.8 m) **Spread:** 12–24" (30–60 cm) **Hardiness:** zones 4–8

Rush

Juncus

Rush is often mistaken for a grass. The stems are hollow and cylindrical rather than flat and broad like grass leaves. This unique plant is a must for any water-related garden.

Growing

Rush grows best in **sun** or **partial shade**. The soil should be **consistently moist if not wet**, and **slightly acidic**.

Tips

Rush is well suited to bog gardens, water gardens and locations that remain moist for long periods. It can be grown in a small container and/or submerged in water up to the crown in a water feature or pond.

Recommended

J. effusus (rush) is a perennial, clump-forming, wetland plant that has slightly arching stems and spreads by vigorous underground rhizomes. The following cultivars are generally smaller than the species, less invasive and hardy to zone 4. **'Cuckoo'** has longitudinal yellow stripes. **'Spiralis'** (corkscrew rush) is low-growing rush with curly, spiraling stems. **'Unicorn'** is an exaggerated version of 'Spiralis,' with thicker, longer, curled stems. **'Zebrinus'** has broad white bands.

'Spiralis' (above & below)

Rush cultivars can overwinter outdoors in the colder areas of our region if they are buried in a well-protected, moist area and covered with several inches of bark mulch or leaf matter. They can also be brought indoors and treated as houseplants until they return outdoors in spring.

Features: foliage, form **Height:** 12"–4' (30 cm–1.2 m) **Spread:** 12–36" (30–90 cm) **Hardiness:** zones 2–9

Sedge
Carex

'Frosted Curls' (above), *C. morrowii* 'Variegata' (below)

"Sedges have edges" is the opening line to a classic gardener's poem that describes this plant as having triangular stems, unlike the true grasses. Sedge foliage comes in green, blue, rust, bronze and gold, and allows the gardener to add broad, colorful strokes or bright accents to the landscape.

Growing
Most sedges grow well in **full sun to part shade** in **moist, well-drained, neutral to slightly alkaline** soil. 'Frosted Curls' prefers average to dry soil and is drought tolerant once established. Propagate by seed or division of clumps in mid-spring to early summer.

Tips
Use the colorful foliage and rustic texture of these grass-like plants in rock gardens, water features, containers and borders. The fine foliage of 'Frosted Curls' contrasts well with coarse-textured plants.

Stems can be cut to the ground in early spring before new growth occurs, or they can be 'combed' to remove older foliage.

Recommended
There are many sedges available; check your local garden center. *C. comans* **'Frosted Curls'** (*C.* 'Frosted Curls'; New Zealand hair sedge) is a compact, clump-forming, evergreen perennial with fine-textured, very pale green, weeping foliage. The foliage appears almost iridescent, with unusual curled and twisted tips.

Features: interesting, colorful foliage; growth habit **Height:** 10–18" (20–45 cm) **Spread:** 12–15" (30–38 cm) **Hardiness:** zones 7–9 (sedge may grow successfully in zone 6, given favorable conditions)

Glossary

Acid soil: soil with a pH lower than 7.0

Annual: a plant that germinates, flowers, sets seed and dies in one growing season

Alkaline soil: soil with a pH higher than 7.0

Basal leaves: leaves that form from the crown, at the base of the plant

Bract: a modified leaf at the base of a flower or flower cluster

Corm: a bulblike, food-storing, underground stem, resembling a bulb without scales

Crown: the part of the plant at or just below soil level where the shoots join the roots

Cultivar: a cultivated plant variety with one or more distinct differences from the species, e.g., in flower color or disease resistance

Damping off: fungal disease causing seedlings to rot at soil level and topple over

Deadhead: to remove spent flowers to maintain a neat appearance and encourage a longer blooming season

Direct sow: to sow seeds directly in the garden

Dormancy: a period of plant inactivity, usually during winter or unfavorable conditions

Double flower: a flower with an unusually large number of petals

Genus: a category of biological classification between the species and family levels; the first word in a scientific name indicates the genus

Grafting: a type of propagation in which a stem or bud of one plant is joined onto the rootstock of another plant of a closely related species

Hardy: capable of surviving unfavorable conditions, such as cold weather or frost, without protection

Hip: the fruit of a rose, containing the seeds

Humus: decomposed or decomposing organic material in the soil

Hybrid: a plant resulting from natural or human-induced cross-breeding between varieties, species or genera

Inflorescence: a flower cluster

Neutral soil: soil with a pH of 7.0

Perennial: a plant that takes three or more years to complete its life cycle

pH: a measure of acidity or alkalinity; the soil pH influences availability of nutrients for plants

Rhizome: a root-like, food-storing stem that grows horizontally at or just below soil level, from which new shoots may emerge

Rootball: the root mass and surrounding soil of a plant

Seedhead: dried, inedible fruit that contains seeds; the fruiting stage of the inflorescense

Self-seeding: reproducing by means of seeds without human assistance, so that new plants constantly replace those that die

Semi-double flower: a flower with petals in two or three rings

Single flower: a flower with a single ring of typically four or five petals

Species: the fundamental unit of biological classification; the entity from which cultivars and varieties are derived

Standard: a shrub or small tree grown with an erect main stem, accomplished either through pruning and training or by grafting the plant onto a tall, straight stock

Sucker: a shoot that comes up from the root, often some distance from the plant; it can be separated to form a new plant once it develops its own roots

Tender: incapable of surviving the climatic conditions of a given region and requiring protection from frost or cold

Tuber: the thick section of a rhizome bearing nodes and buds

Variegation: foliage that has more than one color, often patched or striped or bearing leaf margins of a different color

Variety: a naturally occurring variant of a species

Index of Common Names & Genera